ASK ME ANYTHING ABOUT BASEBALL

LOUIS PHILLIPS is the author of dozens of books for young people, including *Ask Me Anything About the Presidents*. He lives in New York City with his family, where he has a choice of two baseball teams for which to root.

ASK ME ANYTHING ABOUT BASEBALL

LOUIS PHILLIPS

Illustrated by Valerie Costantino

AN AVON CAMELOT BOOK

ASK ME ANYTHING ABOUT BASEBALL is an original publication of Avon Books. This work has never before appeared in book form.

AVON BOOKS
A division of
The Hearst Corporation
1350 Avenue of the Americas
New York, New York 10019

Copyright © 1995 by Louis Phillips
Interior illustrations copyright © 1995 by Avon Books
Illustrations by Valerie Costantino
Published by arrangement with the author
Library of Congress Catalog Card Number: 94-31034
ISBN: 0-380-78029-1
RL: 6.7

Library of Congress Cataloging in Publication Data:

Phillips, Louis.
  Ask me anything about baseball / Louis Phillips.
    p.   cm.
1. Baseball—United States—Miscellanea—Juvenile literature.
[1. Baseball—Miscellanea.] I. Title.
GV867.5.P45 1995   94-31034
796.357'0973—dc20   CIP
                                                                AC

First Avon Camelot Printing: March 1995

CAMELOT TRADEMARK REG. U.S. PAT. OFF. AND IN OTHER COUNTRIES, MARCA REGISTRADA, HECHO EN U.S.A.

Printed in the U.S.A.

OPM   10 9 8 7 6 5 4 3 2

For Ian and Matthew,
my two favorite players

"... one reason I have always loved baseball so much is that it has been not merely 'the great national game,' but really a part of the whole weather of our lives, of the thing that it is our own, of the whole fabric, the million memories of America."

THOMAS WOLFE

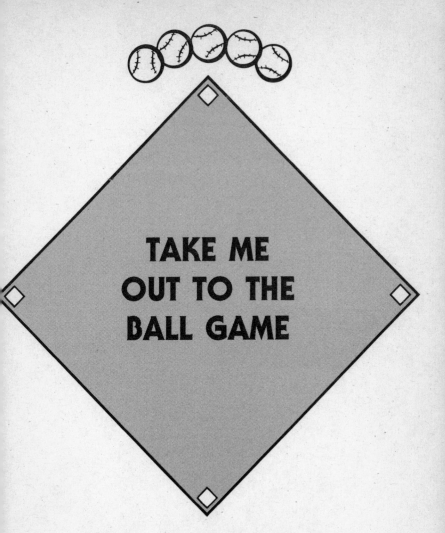

TAKE ME
OUT TO THE
BALL GAME

Things You Didn't Know
About Baseball

When we go to a baseball game, at the seventh-inning stretch, the fans stand up and sing "Take Me Out to the Ballgame." When was the song written and who wrote it?

The words to "Take Me Out to the Ballgame" were written by Jack Northworth in 1908 and the music was composed by Albert Von Tilzer. The strangest thing about the song is that before writing the lyrics Jack Norworth (whose real name was John Klem) had never seen a major league baseball game in his life!

In 1893, what strange rule did Harry Wright, manager of the undefeated 1869 Cincinnati Red Stockings, try to introduce to the game?

Wright figured it would be a good idea if umpires kept the ball/strike count secret until the batter's time at the plate had concluded. He thought that such a rule would increase the offense.

3

What was "Buck's bib"?

The best protector used today by catchers was once called "Buck's bib" in reference to Buck Ewing who introduced that piece of playing equipment to the game.

Buck Ewing, who is in the Baseball Hall of Fame, played major league ball for eighteen years (from 1880 through 1897, although he appeared in only one game in his final season). For most of his career he played with the New York Giants. Ewing was one of the most versatile players the game has ever seen, appearing in 1,315 games as a catcher, outfielder, first baseman, second baseman, shortstop, and third baseman. He batted for a lifetime average of .303, and even pitched in nine games. In one game, he started as the catcher, and then, when his team fell behind, he took over as the pitcher and won the game!

When and where was the first night game played?

The first night game was played at Ebbets Field in Brooklyn on June 15, 1933. Cincinnati's pitcher beat the Dodgers on a no-hitter.

What is "blue mud" and what does it have to do with baseball?

New baseballs have to be rubbed with mud in order to rid them of gloss. The mud used in the major leagues comes from the banks of a creek near the Delaware River, and each major league team buys about fifteen pounds of the stuff per year. The mud was first used by the American League in 1938; the National League started using the mud in 1955.

Why is the pitching/catching combination known as "the Battery"?

It refers to military artillery. Henry Chadwick, in his 1897 book, *Technical Terms of Baseball,* stated that "the Battery is the term applied to both the pitcher and catcher of a team. It is the main attacking force of the little army of nine players in the field in a contest."

When did it happen that two pitchers were sent to jail because they refused to pitch?

That strange incident took place during spring training of 1947. The New York Yankees were in Caracas, Venezuela and were playing the Vargas club. Earlier that year, two pitchers for Vargas—Ed Chandler and George Brown—were purchased by the Brooklyn Dodgers, and Dodger general manager Branch Rickey told them not to pitch after February 28. The game between the Yankees and Vargas took place on March 1. The local promoter of the exhibition match charged that he had paid both hurlers to appear in the exhibition games, and, because they were committing a breach of contract, the promoter had both pitchers arrested and hauled off to the local jail.

The Yankees, by the way, lost the game 4–3.

What was the first baseball game to charge admission?

In 1857, when the All Star New York played Brooklyn at Fashion Race Course on Long Island, admission was charged for the very first time. The cost to see the game was 50 cents—not exactly cheap in those days.

When were the first baseball cards issued?

The first baseball card set consisted of ten players included in the fifty-card set Allen & Ginter issued in 1887. These cards were distributed in cigarette packs, and among the players represented was Mike "King" Kelly, one of the more popular players of his day.

Today, the home plate umpire always stands behind the catcher. Did the homeplate umpire always stand?

No. In the very early days of baseball (before 1859, to be exact) the home-plate umpire sat in a padded rocking chair. The rocking chair, however, turned out to be too much of a hindrance. Besides who wants an umpire to get too comfortable during the game?

Is it true that a ballplayer once caught a baseball that had been tossed off the top of the Washington Monument in Washington, D.C.?

It is a very foolish and dangerous stunt, but it has in fact been done. On August 21, 1908, to win a $500 bet, Charles Street caught a regulation baseball dropped 550 feet from the observation window of the Washington Monument. Before Street accomplished the feat, several other catchers such as Paul Himes, Charley Snyder, and Buck Ewing had tried and failed. It was estimated that the ball was going slightly more than 140 feet per second. Street caught it on the 14th attempt. Not only did the catcher have to reckon with the speed of the baseball, he had to take into account a strong breeze. The ball struck the catcher's mitt with such force that the "whack" could be heard several hundred yards away.

Seven years later, on March 13, 1915, Brooklyn Dodgers manager Wilbert Robinson tried to catch a baseball from an airplane. The pilot, however, to play a joke, substituted a grapefruit for the baseball. When Robinson tried to catch it, the grapefruit splattered all over him.

In 1931, Cleveland player Joe Sprinz caught a ball dropped 800 feet from an airship. The ball, however, broke Sprinz's jaw.

When Charles A. Lindbergh became the first person to fly solo across the Atlantic Ocean in his plane, the Spirit of St. Louis, what honor did major league baseball confer upon him?

In June of 1927, in ceremonies conducted at Sportsman Park in St. Louis, Colonel Charles A. Lindbergh was presented by the National League with a solid gold pass entitling him to free entry to all National League ballgames. He was only the third person to receive such an honor. The two other honorees were President Calvin Coolidge and Governor Al Smith of New York.

When the great pitcher for the Washington Senators, Walter Johnson, became the manager of the Newark International League club, he formulated twelve theories for managing. What were they?

Walter Johnson's rules for managing were:

1. Every player must hustle every minute. No athlete who loafs will be kept in the lineup.
2. Every player will be treated individually. Those who need coaxing will be coaxed. Those who need driving will be invited to follow orders.
3. No player will be scolded for mechanical errors. These are part of the game.
4. No player will cheat with Walter Johnson's knowledge or consent. That is, pitchers will not be allowed to roughen the ball or use any substance to make the ball do tricks.
5. No rowdyism or useless arguing with fans or umpires will be tolerated. Suspended athletes are a dead loss to the club.
6. Every player will be allowed, generally speaking, to use his own judgment until he proves he can't think for himself. This will apply to pitchers, base runners, and others.
7. No player's natural-batting or pitching style will be changed.

8. No attempt will be made by Johnson to signal for the various balls to be pitched, to give orders for every play.

9. Every player will be expected to practice to correct any weakness he shows.

10. Every player must obey orders and practice self-control.

11. Every player will be told to forget alibis and talk and think of victory. Believing in yourself is one of Walter's pet theories.

12. Fight for every game as if the pennant depended on it. But don't fight with players of your own club, no matter what the provocation.

On the football field, referees, because of their black-and-white striped shirts, are sometimes facetiously referred to as "zebras." Has any baseball team ever introduced black-and-white striped uniforms?

Yes. In 1911, manager John J. McGraw of the New York Giants introduced the idea of wearing a white uniform with black perpendicular stripes and black caps, black belt, and black-and-white stockings. It was, however, the custom in the National League for teams to wear white or cream-colored uniforms at all home games, so Mr. McGraw's idea never caught on.

Has a major league game ever been called off because of too many insects on the field?

Yes, that has happened at least once. On September 15, 1946, the Brooklyn Dodgers were playing the Chicago Cubs at Wrigley Field in Chicago. The game was called at the end of five innings because of gnats. The swarms of gnats were causing such problems for the players, umpires, and fans, that the game was halted, with the Dodgers leading 2–0.

Has a former president of the United States ever managed a baseball team?

Not really, but in 1961, during spring training, Dwight David Eisenhower managed the Los Angeles Angels (as they were then called) for the middle innings of one game.

Has a major league game ever been played without an infielder being credited with an assist?

Strange as it may be, it has happened ten times in the entire history of the game that a club has played nine innings and not recorded one infield assist. The last time it happened was on September 12, 1993, when Sid Fernandez of the New York Mets shut out the Cubs 5–0. The Met infielders had no assists. Fernandez also is the only pitcher in National League history to pitch a game that required no assists of any kind! Fernandez accomplished that feat on June 25, 1989, against the Phillies.

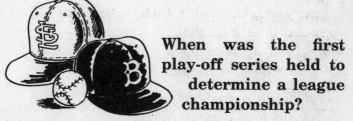

When was the first play-off series held to determine a league championship?

In October of 1946, a play-off series—the first one in major league history—was held to determine the winner of the National League pennant. The St. Louis Cardinals played the Brooklyn Dodgers.

Could you tell me who wrote the immortal poem "Casey at the Bat"?

It was written by Ernest Lawrence Thayer. The entire poem, the most famous ever written about baseball, is fun to read and to recite aloud:

Casey at the Bat

*The outlook wasn't brilliant
    for the Mudville nine that day;
The score stood four to two with but
    one inning more to play.
And then, when Cooney died at first,
    and Barrows did the same,
A sickly silence fell upon the patrons of the game.*

*A straggling few got up to go in deep despair.
The rest clung to that hope which springs
    eternal in the human breast;
They thought, If only Casey could but
    get a whack at that
We'd put up even money now,
    with Casey at the bat.*

*But Flynn preceded Casey,
    as did also Jimmy Blake,
And the former was a lulu and the latter was a cake;
So upon that stricken multitude
    grim melancholy sat,
For there seemed but little chance of Casey's
    getting to the bat.*

14

But Flynn let drive a single,
  to the wonderment of all,
And Blake, the much despised,
  tore the cover off the ball;
And when the dust had lifted,
  and men saw what had occurred,
There was Jimmy safe at second,
  and Flynn a-hugging third.

Then from five thousand throats and more
  there rose a lusty yell;
It rumbled through the valley,
  it rattled in the dell;
It knocked upon the mountain
  and recoiled upon the flat,
For Casey, mighty Casey,
  was advancing to the bat.

There was ease in Casey's manner
  as he stepped into his place;
There was pride in Casey's bearing
  and a smile on Casey's face.
And when, responding to the cheers,
  he lightly doffed his hat,
No stranger in the crowd could doubt 'twas
  Casey at the bat.

Ten thousand eyes were on him
  as he rubbed his hands with dirt,
Five thousand tongues applauded
  when he wiped them on his shirt;

Then while the writhing pitcher
  ground the ball into his hip,
Defiance gleamed from Casey's eye,
  a sneer curled Casey's lip.

And now the leather-covered sphere came
  hurtling through the air,
And Casey stood a-watching it
  in haughty grandeur there.
Close by the sturdy batsman
  the ball unheeded sped;
"That ain't my style," said Casey.
  "Strike one," the umpire said.

From the benches, black with people,
  there went up a muffled roar,
Like the beating of the storm waves
  on a stern and distant shore.
"Kill him! Kill the umpire!"
  shouted someone on the stand;
And it's likely they'd have killed him had not
  Casey raised his hand.

With a smile of Christian charity
  great Casey's visage shone;
He stilled the rising tumult,
  he bade the game go on;
He signaled to the pitcher,
  and once more the spheroid flew;

But Casey still ignored it, and the umpire said,
  "Strike two."

"Fraud!" cried the maddened thousands,
  and echo answered "Fraud!"
But one scornful look from Casey
  and the audience was awed;
They saw his face grow stern and cold,
  they saw his muscles strain,
And they knew that Casey wouldn't let
  that ball go by again.

The sneer is gone from Casey's lip,
  his teeth are clenched in hate,
He pounds with cruel violence
  his bat upon the plate;
And now the pitcher holds the ball,
  and now he lets it go,
And now the air is shattered by
  the force of Casey's blow.

Oh, somewhere in this favored land
  the sun is shining bright,
The band is playing somewhere,
  and somewhere hearts are light;
And somewhere men are laughing,
  and somewhere children shout,
But there is no joy in Mudville—
  mighty Casey has struck out.

What was the name of the Brooklyn National League team before they became known as the Dodgers?

They were called the Brooklyn Bridegrooms, but they were known as the Dodgers (short for the Trolley-Dodgers) because residents of Brooklyn frequently had to "dodge" so many trolleys on the way to Ebbets Field.

Has any team gone from last place in one season to first place the next?

Curiously enough the only time it has happened so far was in 1991 when two teams accomplished that feat—the Atlanta Braves and the Minnesota Twins, both last in 1990, went on to capture their division titles one year later.

Is it possible for a pitcher to enter a game and win it without throwing one pitch to the plate?

Yes, it is possible. Here is one example: Ray Roberts, who played minor league ball for the Erie Team in the Central League in 1928, entered as a reliever in the top of the ninth inning. There was a man on first and two outs. With his first throw, Roberts picked off the runner, retiring the side. The Erie team then came up to bat and won the game. Roberts was declared the winning pitcher.

Who was the last legal spitball pitcher in the American League?

Urban "Red" Faber, who won twenty or more games four times and is a member of baseball's Hall of Fame, was the last legal spitball pitcher in the American League. During the 1917 World Series, Faber pitched for the Chicago White Sox and won three games, one of the few pitchers to accomplish that feat.

What player received the largest cash bonus for signing with a major league team?

Brien Taylor. To get him to sign a contract, the New York Yankees in 1991 offered this left-handed pitcher a cash incentive of $1,550,000. No "Bonus Baby" has ever been paid more.

Is it true that baseball players were once arrested for playing on Sundays?

Yes. Well into the twentieth century, most American cities had "blue laws"—laws stipulating that stores had to be closed on Sunday and no professional sports could be played. For example, on July 29, 1907, the *New York Times* reported that "Eight more arrests for Sunday ball playing were made yesterday. . . . The men arrested are members of the Royal Giants, a colored semi-professional team." The battle to allow baseball playing on Sunday was a long and arduous one, and today Sunday sports events are quite common.

What two-sport wonder became, in 1989, the first pro athlete to hit a major league home run and score an NFL touchdown in the same week?

That remarkable feat was accomplished by Deion Sanders. On September 5, 1989, Deion smashed a home run for the New York Yankees (against the Seattle Mariners) and then on September 10, playing for the Atlanta Falcons in a game against the Los Angeles Rams, he returned a punt 68 yards for an NFL touchdown. Some week!

When was the first baseball game broadcast?

The first baseball game to be broadcast was between the Pittsburgh Pirates and the Philadelphia Phillies. The game, played on August 5, 1921, was aired on radio station KDKA, and the announcer was Harold Arlin. The Pirates won the game 8–5.

What is the most number of extra-inning games played by a team in a single season?

Thirty-one. In 1943, the Boston Red Sox played 31 extra-inning games, winning 15, losing 14, and tying 2. The National League record for extra-inning games, strangely enough, was also set that year when the other Boston team—the Braves—played 27 extra-inning contests. The 1967 Los Angeles Dodgers tied that record of 27 extra-inning National League games.

In what motion picture did movie star Ronald Reagan (who went on to become president of the United States) portray Hall of Fame pitcher Grover Cleveland Alexander?

The film was *The Winning Team,* released in 1952. In the movie numerous real major league players—such as Bob Lemon, Al Zarilla, and George "Catfish" Metkovich—can also be seen.

We all know that the Toronto baseball team is known as the Blue Jays, but what were some of the other names that were suggested for Toronto's ball club?

In 1976, a contest was held to name the Toronto major league baseball club. More than 30,000 entries were submitted. Some of the names suggested were: Blue Bats, Maple Leafs, Bootleggers, Hogtowners, and Blue Sox. Aren't you glad that the officials chose Blue Jays over Hogtowners?

Has any major league pitcher ever lost a perfect game on the 27th batter?

Alas! Yes. Think how Detroit pitcher Tommy Bridges must have felt on August 5, 1931, when he entered the ninth inning with a perfect game against the hapless Washington Senators. Bridges retired the first two batters and he had only one more batter to go. The twenty-seventh batter (a pinch hitter named Dave Harris), however, blooped a single and the masterpiece was ruined.

What outfielder once played center field in his stocking feet during a thunderstorm?

Willie Tasby of the Baltimore Orioles. He was afraid that the spikes on his shoes would attract lightning.

What is the most times a player has homered from both sides of the plate in the same game?

When it comes to switch hitters, two of the most powerful were Mickey Mantle and Eddie Murray. In his career, Mantle homered from both sides of the plate in 10 games. His record stood until 1994, when Eddie Murray moved ahead of him. As of this writing, Murray accomplished that feat 11 times.

Has any major league player ever won the batting title in one league while he was playing for the other league?

Incredibly enough, it has happened. In 1990, Willie McGee won the National League batting title as a member of the Oakland Athletics in the American League, because on August 28, while batting .335, he was traded to the Athletics from the St. Louis Cardinals. McGee won the batting title when Dave Magadan of the New York Mets failed to overtake him on the final game of the season.

What was the biggest trade in baseball history?

In terms of the number of players involved, the biggest trade in baseball history took place on November 18, 1954, between the Baltimore Orioles and the New York Yankees. Eighteen— count 'em—eighteen—players were traded. One of the players involved in that monumental swap was no other than Don Larsen, the player who went on to pitch the only perfect game in World Series history.

Who invented the pitching machine?

I suppose the answer to that question depends on what kind of pitching machine is being referred to, but certainly one of the inventors who should be given special mention is Alexander MacMillan, the son of a Princeton University professor. Back in 1914, MacMillan invented a machine that consisted of a throwing arm of steel pivoted in a frame, with fingers attached to one end and a strong spring to the other.

According to a newspaper account of the day, "The machine delivers to the batter any number of regulation balls, as fast as one in every eight seconds if the batter wants them that fast. Every one passes directly over the plate, and the height and speed at which they can be thrown is regulated by the lever which a man works behind the batter, on the same principle as the clay pigeon throwing machine."

Where is Babe Ruth buried?

The Great Bambino is buried at the Gate of Heaven Cemetery in Mount Pleasant, New York.

Which United States president attended the most baseball games while in office?

Harry S Truman was probably the biggest presidential baseball fan. While he was in office, he attended some 16 games. Taft went 14 times, and Eisenhower saw 13 games. Wilson, Roosevelt, and Nixon each attended 11 games.

How many players have played for a losing team and yet still were voted their league's Most Valuable Player?

Only three players in baseball history have been named MVP as part of a losing team. They are: Ernie Banks of the Chicago Cubs (1958, 1959), Andre Dawson of the Chicago Cubs (1987), and Cal Ripken of the Baltimore Orioles (1991).

In *Sport Magazine* for December 1954, Ted Williams gave some advice about hitting. What did he say?

"The Splendid Splinter" (a nickname he received because he was as thin as a toothpick) was quoted as saying:

1. Hit only strikes.
2. Never swing at a ball you've been fooled on or have trouble hitting.
3. After two strikes, concede the long ball to the pitcher, shorten up on the bat, and try to put the head of the bat on the ball.

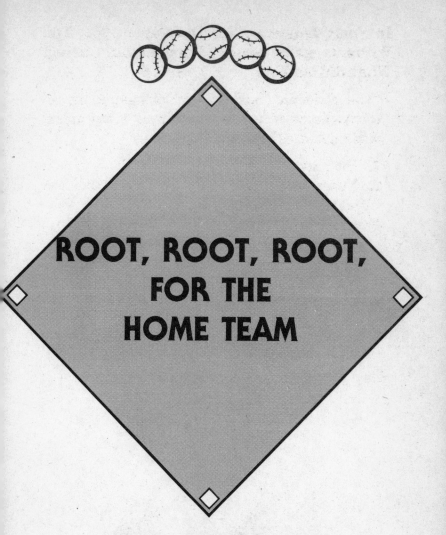

ROOT, ROOT, ROOT, FOR THE HOME TEAM

People You Did and Didn't Know About in Baseball

Who was Alma Ziegler, and why was she called "the Hitless Wonder"?

Alma Ziegler was a member of the All-American Girls Professional Baseball League (AAGPBL). She was the captain of the Grand Rapids Chicks, where she played second base and pitched. She was called "the Hitless Wonder" because the best she ever hit in a single season was .183, and her lifetime batting average was only .173, and yet she was a tremendous fielder and an outstanding pitcher. In 1950, for example, she won 19 games, lost 7, and compiled an amazing 1.36 earned run average. In that same year she was named the AAGPBL Player of the Year. A baseball card was recently issued in her honor by the Ted Williams Card Company.

A film about the Girls Professional Baseball League—*A League of Their Own*—helped revive interest in the role of women in professional baseball.

What noted baseball player was "born to be a Met"?

Marvin Eugene Throneberry, because of his initials.

In 1927, Babe Ruth signed a three-year contract with the New York Yankees. How much was "the Great Bambino" paid?

In 1926, Ruth tore into American League pitching. He finished the season with a .372 batting average, 47 home runs, and 145 runs batted in. With a new contract called for, Ruth requested an unprecedented $100,000 per year. Colonel Jack Ruppert, owner of the Yankees, had a fit. After much negotiation, Ruth settled for a three-year contract for $210,000 or $70,000 per year. By today's standards that may not seem like a lot of money for a baseball superstar, but you have to remember that money went a bit further then. And, $70,000 per year was the highest baseball salary of its day. At the time, Ty Cobb was earning $60,000 per season, and the great Tris Speaker was being paid $40,000.

By point of contrast, in the 1880s, Buck Ewing of the New York Giants earned $5,000 per season. In 1896, when Honus Wagner signed with the Paterson Club of the Atlantic League, presided over by Ed Barrow, he received $2,100 per season. The next year Wagner joined the Louisville Club of the National League and got a $500 raise.

When Ruth signed his 1927 contract, the *New York Times* described it as "the most valuable baseball document ever executed," and went on to say that Ruth's $70,000 salary was "just a trifle more than seven times the entire yearly salary of the original Cincinnati Club, which had a roster of ten players. The highest salaried player on that team was George Wright, who was signed for $1,400 for the season."

Commenting on Ruth's $70,000 salary, Colonel Ruppert said: "It's a big gamble with me. But I am convinced that Ruth, a remarkable fellow physically, won't make me sorry."

The Colonel was right.

How did Leroy Paige get the nickname "Satchel"?

He got his nickname from the fact that as a young boy, he carried luggage and satchels at the Mobile railroad station.

Who are baseball's all-time strike-out leaders?

The pitchers who have struck out more batters than any others are:

1. Nolan Ryan—5,714
2. Steve Carlton—4,136
3. Bert Blyleven—3,701
4. Tom Seaver—3,640
5. Don Sutton—3,574
6. Gaylord Perry—3,534
7. Walter Johnson—3,508
8. Phil Niekro—3,342
9. Ferguson Jenkins—3,192
10. Bob Gibson—3,117

Has any major league catcher ever tagged out two runners at home plate on the same play?

It does happen once in a while. For example, on April 29, 1933, Luke Sewell—the catcher for the Washington Senators—tagged out both Lou Gehrig and Dixie Walker. Starting down from third, Lou Gehrig held up because he thought the ball would be caught. Dixie Walker was right behind him, and all Sewell did was tag both runners for a strange double play.

Although there have not been many left-handed catchers in the major leagues, there have been a few. Who was the best left-handed catcher of all time?

The best of the left-handed catchers was probably a player named Jack Clements. Playing from 1884–1900, mostly for the Philadelphia Phillies, Clements appeared in 1,157 games (playing 1,073 games as catcher) and had a lifetime batting average of .286. In 1895, for example, Clements came to bat 322 times and hit for a tremendous .394 average, with 13 home runs.

What major league pitcher came the closest to equaling Johnny Vander Meer's great feat of pitching two consecutive no-hit games?

A few pitchers have come close, but the honor goes to Ewell "the Whip" Blackwell. On June 18, 1947, Blackwell, pitching for the Cincinnati Reds against the Boston Braves, tossed a no-hitter. His next start was four days later, on June 22nd, against the Brooklyn Dodgers. The Whip had a no-hitter for 8 and $\frac{1}{3}$d innings until the Dodgers finally got a hit off him.

What major league player entered the world of baseball legend by refusing to take three strikes against Walter Johnson?

That player was George Harper of the Cincinnati Reds. Playing against the Washington Senators in a spring-training game in 1922, he came to the plate to face the superb fastball pitcher Walter Johnson ("the Big Train"). Harper took two quick strikes and then turned to walk back to the dugout.

"Wait," the umpire said to Harper. "You still have one strike left."

But Harper, shaken by the speed of the pitches, replied, "I don't want it," and decided to seek the safety of the Reds dugout.

Who was the only major-leaguer to hit .300, drive in 100 runs, score 100 runs, hit 30 homers, and steal 50 bases in a single season?

Barry Bonds of the Pittsburgh Pirates. In 1990 he hit .301, scored 104 runs, drove in 114 runs, hit 33 home runs, and stole 52 bases. Some players don't accomplish that in a lifetime.

Have any brothers, during their first season in the majors, ever faced each other as opposing pitchers?

Yes. On September 29, 1986, Chicago Cub rookie Greg Maddux opposed his brother Mike, who was the pitcher for the Philadelphia Phillies. It may have been the first time that brothers faced each other as rookie pitchers. The Cubs won 8–3.

What feat did Joe Tinker of the Chicago Cubs accomplish on June 28, 1910?

On that date, Joe Tinker (of the famed double-play combination Tinker to Evers to Chance) became the first major-leaguer to steal home twice in the same game.

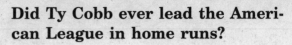

Did Ty Cobb ever lead the American League in home runs?

Yes. In 1909, "the Georgia Peach" took the home-run title, when he slugged a whopping nine round-trippers. It was the only year that Cobb led the league in homers.

What major league manager, in order to increase baseball's offense, once suggested that the batter be given four strikes instead of three?

Connie Mack of the Philadelphia Athletics. Back in 1910, Mack believed that four strikes and four balls would be more effective in placing the batter on equal footing with the pitcher. He also advocated that fouls not be counted as strikes.

The foul-strike rule, by the way, was adopted to prevent the batter from fouling off good balls in order to get to first base on called balls. Mike Kelly was one of the players who fouled off ball after ball before finally getting a walk to first.

Has any player hit more than 400 home runs and yet not been elected to baseball's Hall of Fame?

Unfortunately, yes. Dave Kingman, who played for sixteen years (1971–1986) on such teams as the San Francisco Giants, the New York Mets, the Chicago Cubs, and the Oakland Athletics, clubbed 442 home runs, but he is not a member of baseball's Hall of Fame. Although he hit home runs (he led the National League in 1979 with 48 homers and in 1982 with 37), "Kong" (as he was nicknamed) struck out a lot (1,816 times in his career) and never hit higher than .288 in a full season. His lifetime batting average was only .236.

Other players who have hit more than 375 home runs and have not been elected to the Hall of Fame include Graig Nettles (390 homers), Frank Howard (382), Orlando Cepeda (379), Tony Perez (379), and Norm Cash (377).

Who is the only major-leaguer to win batting titles in three different decades?

George Brett of the Kansas City Royals. He won batting titles in 1976, 1980, and 1990.

Who was the first pitcher in the major leagues to win, in the same season, both the Most Valuable Player Award and the Cy Young Award?

Dennis McLain of the Detroit Tigers in 1968. In that year, McLain won 31 games and lost 6. McLain, by the way, married Sharyn Alice Boudreau, the daughter of Hall of Famer Lou Boudreau.

Captain Hook is a favorite character in *Peter Pan*. Who in the major leagues was called "Captain Hook"?

Sparky Anderson, because during his years as manager of the Cincinnati Reds, he was very quick to give "the hook" to (that is, to remove) the starting pitchers in his rotation.

What hitting feat did George Brett of the Kansas City Royals accomplish from May 8 through May 13, 1976?

George Howard Brett got three or more hits in each of those six games, setting a major league record for most consecutive games for getting three or more hits per game.

Who was Satchel Paige talking about when he said this player "was so fast, he could switch off the light and be in bed before the room got dark?"

Satchel Paige was describing "Cool Papa" Bell, who was sometimes called the fastest man ever to play baseball. There are stories of him stealing second and third on the same pitch! Bell played from 1922 to 1946, but because he was black, he never got a chance to play in the major leagues. Bell is, however, a member of baseball's Hall of Fame.

Could you please tell me something about Frank Robinson, and why he is important to the history of baseball?

When he joined the Cleveland Indians in 1975 as a player-manager, he became the first black manager in the history of the major leagues.

Frank Robinson was born August 31, 1935, in Beaumont, Texas, and joined the Cincinnati Reds in 1956, batting .290 and leading the National League in runs scored with 122. He slugged 38 home runs that year, setting a new record for home runs by a rookie. The following year he raised his batting average to .322, with 29 homers. From 1956 to 1967, Robinson hit 20 home runs each season, his high being 49 in 1966 with the Baltimore Orioles. Of his 586 career home runs, he hit 343 in the National League and 243 in the American.

Who were the first black siblings to play major league baseball?

In 1884, Fleet and Welday Walker both played for the Toledo Blue Stockings of the American Association. Toledo at that time was considered to be a major league franchise.

In the years from 1962 to 1968 inclusive, who was the only pitcher in either league to pitch more than 200 innings in each of seven consecutive seasons?

Dean Chance of the Minnesota Twins and the Los Angeles Angels (as the team was then called). In 1964, he won 20 games, of which 11 were shutouts. His ERA that year was 1.65, the lowest earned run average in the majors since 1940.

Who was the oldest pitcher ever to pitch in the majors?

Leroy "Satchel" Paige. In 1965, Satchel, at the age of 59 (some claim he was even older) Paige pitched three innings for the Kansas City Athletics. He allowed only one hit.

What Hall of Fame pitcher, with more than 300 career wins and 2,000 strike-outs to his credit, never once led his league in either wins, strike-outs, or ERA?

That was Eddie Plank. He did, however, lead the American League in 1903 in number of games started (40) and number of games pitched (43). In 1905, he led the American League in games started (41) and complete games (36). In his 17-year career, "Gettysburg Eddie" (so called because he was born in Gettysburg, Pennsylvania, on August 31, 1875) won 327 games, lost 193, and compiled a remarkable 2.43 ERA.

What father and son duo, who both pitched in the major leagues, allowed home runs to Ted Williams?

Thornton Lee and Don Lee. Thorton Lee (1933–1948) won 117 games and lost 124. His son Don, who pitched from 1957–1966, won 40 games and lost 44.

Most baseball fans are well aware that Joe DiMaggio's 56-game hitting streak is a major league record, but what player holds the hitting-streak record for rookies?

In 1987, Benito Santiago, playing his first season with the San Diego Padres, hit safely in 34 consecutive games to set the rookie record. His streak came to a halt on October 3d of that year, when the Padres, snapping a 9-game losing streak, beat the Dodgers 1–0.

Has anyone ever played for the New York Yankees, the New York Giants, *and* the Brooklyn Dodgers?

Yes. Second baseman Tony "Poosh 'em up" Lazzeri is the only player to have played for those three major New York baseball teams. He played most of his career with the New York Yankees, but in 1939, Lazzeri played 14 games for the Dodgers and 13 games for the Giants.

What baseball Hall of Famer once said of his looks—"So I'm ugly. So what? I never saw anyone hit with his face."

That is Yogi Berra at his finest.

How did James "Orator Jim" O'Rourke get his nickname?

O'Rourke, who played from 1876 to 1904, and who was elected to baseball's Hall of Fame in 1945, got his nickname from the fact that he had attended Yale Law School and was known for his flowery speeches. At the age of 52, O'Rourke caught a 9-inning game for the New York Giants—making him the oldest player ever to catch in the big leagues. His son— Queenie O'Rourke—played briefly for the 1908 New York American League team.

Who holds the major league record for grounding into the most double plays in a single season?

Jim Rice, outfielder for the Boston Red Sox. In 1984, in 159 games, Rice grounded into 36 double plays.

The National League record of 30 was set by Ernest N. Lombardi, catcher for the Cincinnati Reds, in 1938.

What player is credited with being the first to hit a home run?

That baseball milestone is credited to Roscoe C. Barnes. Playing with Chicago in the National League, he hit the first major league home run on May 2, 1876.

Erwin T. Beck of Cleveland is credited with the first American League home run hit on April 25, 1901.

What player hit more grand slams than any other?

Lou Gehrig. He hit 23 home runs with the bases loaded. Willie McCovey, with 17 grand slams, ranks second.

Who is Sadaharu Oh?

Sadaharu Oh was a professional baseball player for the Yomiuri Giants in Japan who hit more home runs than any person in the game. His lifetime total of 868 homers surpasses the totals of Aaron and Ruth, and his home runs came in 9,250 at bats, as opposed to 12,364 at bats for Aaron and 8,399 at bats for Ruth.

In 1974, Oh slugged 49 home runs in only 385 at bats. During his career, which spanned the early 1960s until the mid 1970s, Oh won 15 home-run titles and 13 RBI crowns.

Although a number of fathers and sons have played in the major leagues, has any father-and-son combination ever played at the same time for the same team?

Yes. Ken Griffey played with his son Ken Griffey, Jr., for the Seattle Mariners. In fact, on September 24, 1990, Ken Griffey and Ken Griffey, Jr., hit consecutive homers in the first inning of a game against the California Angels—the only time that father/son feat has been accomplished. Both homers came off pitcher Kirk McCaskill.

Who was the oldest rookie in Major League history?

Satchel Paige. When he joined the 1948 Cleveland Indians, he was at least 42 years old.

Who was the first pitcher in history to strike out 15 batters in his very first major league appearance?

Karl Spooner of the Brooklyn Dodgers. On September 22, 1954, he made his major league debut against the New York Giants and struck out 15 batters, winning 3–0.

Many fathers and sons have played baseball in the major leagues. Which father/son combination hit more home runs than any other?

Barry Bonds and his father Bobby Bonds have hit 509 home runs, the most by a father/son combination. In addition, Barry and his father are the only father/son tandem to win Gold Glove awards.

Has any major league baseball player ever "hit for the cycle" in both leagues?

When a player hits a home run, a triple, a double, and a single in the same game, he is said to have "hit for the cycle." The first player to accomplish that feat in both leagues was Bob Watson of the Boston Red Sox. On September 15, 1979, he hit for the cycle when Boston defeated the Baltimore Orioles by the score of 10–2. He had previously hit for the cycle in the National League on June 24, 1977, when he played for the Houston Astros in a game against the San Francisco Giants.

What major league pitcher, with 100 or more victories, has the highest winning percentage?

Spurgeon "Spud" Chandler, who pitched from 1937–1947, chalked up 109 wins against 43 defeats. His .717 winning percentage is the highest of all major league pitchers who have won at least 100 games. Second is Whitey Ford of the New York Yankees. From 1950–1967, Whitey won 236 and lost 106 for a .690 winning percentage.

Has any pitcher ever pitched both games in a doubleheader and shut out the opposing team in both games?

Yes. Such a feat has been accomplished just one time in the majors. On September 26, 1911, Ed Reulbach of the Chicago Cubs became the only pitcher to throw 2 shutouts in a doubleheader. He beat the Dodgers 5–0 in the first game and 3–0 in the second. Both games went 9 innings.

In how many games did Babe Ruth hit 2 or more home runs?

Seventy-two games. Willie Mays accomplished that feat 63 times; Hank Aaron 62 times.

Has any player ever hit a home run in his very first major league at bat?

Yes. Quite a few in fact. In 1992, Jim Bullinger, of the Chicago Cubs, hit a home run on the very first pitch ever thrown to him in the majors. Below is a list of the players who have hit homers in their first major league at bat:

American Association

George Tebeau
Cincinnati, 1887

Mike Griffin
Baltimore, 1887

National League

Bill Duggleby
Philadelphia, 1898

Johnny Bates
Boston, 1906

Walter Mueller
Pittsburgh, 1922

Clise Dudley
Brooklyn, 1929

Gordon Slade
Brooklyn, 1930

Eddie Morgan
St. Louis, 1936

Ernie Koy
Brooklyn, 1938

Emmett Mueller
Philadelphia, 1938

Clyde Vollmer
Cincinnati, 1942

Buddy Kerr
New York, 1943

Whitey Lockman
New York, 1945

Dan Bankhead
Brooklyn, 1947

Les Layton
New York, 1948

Ed Sanicki
Philadelphia, 1949

Ted Tappe
Cincinnati, 1950

Hoyt Wilhelm
New York, 1952

Wally Moon
St. Louis, 1954

Chuck Tanner
Milwaukee, 1955

Bill White
New York, 1956

Frank Ernaga
Chicago, 1957

Don Leppert
Pittsburgh, 1961

Cuno Barragan
Chicago, 1961

Bennie Ayala
New York, 1974
John Montefusco
San Francisco, 1974
Jose Sosa
Houston, 1975
Johnnie LeMaster
San Francisco, 1975
Carmelo Martinez
Chicago, 1983
Mike Fitzgerald
New York, 1983

Will Clark
San Francisco, 1986
Ricky Jordan
Philadelphia, 1988
Jose Offerman
Los Angeles, 1990
Dave Elland
San Diego, 1992
Jim Bullinger
Chicago, 1992

American League

Earl Averill
Cleveland, 1929
Ace Parker
Philadelphia, 1937
Bill LeFebvre
Boston, 1938
Hack Miller
Detroit, 1944
Eddie Pellagrini
Boston, 1946
George Vico
Detroit, 1948
Bob Nieman
St. Louis, 1951
Bob Tillman
Boston, 1962
John Kennedy
Washington, 1962
Buster Narum
Baltimore, 1963
Gates Brown
Detroit, 1963

Bert Campaneris
Kansas City, 1964
Bill Roman
Detroit, 1964.
Brant Alyea
Washington, 1965
John Miller
New York, 1966
Rick Renick
Minnesota, 1968
Joe Keough
Oakland, 1968
Gene Lamont
Detroit, 1970
Don Rose
California, 1972
Reggie Sanders
Detroit, 1974
Dave McKay
Minnesota, 1975

Has any pitcher in the All-Star Game ever won the Most Valuable Player (MVP) award without being the winning pitcher?

Yes. It has happened once, and only once. It happened in the 1965 All-Star Game. The All-Star Game MVP was Juan Marichal. He started the game and pitched three shutout innings, but it was Sandy Koufax, who pitched one inning in relief, who actually got the victory.

When Joe DiMaggio's brother Dominic led the American League in stolen bases in 1950, how many bases did he steal?

Dom DiMaggio, outfielder for the Boston Red Sox, stole all of 15 bases that year, and it was enough to lead the league!

Who was the only starting player in the 1934 All-Star Game who is not a member of Baseball's Hall of Fame?

Wally Berger, who started at center field for the National League, is the only starting member of either team who has not been elected to the Hall of Fame.

What major league player slugged 200 home runs in the fewest number of times at bat? Was it Babe Ruth? Or Hank Aaron?

You might think Ruth or Aaron would be the players to accomplish the feat of hitting 200 home runs in the fewest at bats, but, in point of fact, the honor belongs to Ralph Kiner, who hit his 200th home run in only 2,537 at bats. It took Ruth 2,580 at bats to achieve his 200th homer. Only one other player hit 200 homers in less than 2,600 at bats and that was Harmon Killebrew of the old Washington Senators and the Minnesota Twins. Killebrew hit 200 homers in 2,584 at bats, which was only 4 more at bats than the Babe. Eddie Matthews hit 200 home runs in 2,811 at bats. In 1992, Oakland slugger Mark McGwire joined that illustrious crew when he hit his 200th home run in his 2,852d at bat. McGwire ranks fifth in the all-time list in this category.

How many times was Babe Ruth voted the Most Valuable Player of his league?

Believe it or not, Babe Ruth was never voted MVP. No matter how well he performed, someone, frequently first baseman Jimmy Foxx, always managed to beat him out for that honor.

What dubious feat did John J. Ryan of the Louisville Colonels accomplish on July 22, 1876?

On that date, John J. Ryan, Louisville Colonels' pitcher, hurled 10—count 'em 10—wild pitches in a single game! No pitcher has come close to that mark.

Who is the only major league pitcher to have won 20 games as a starter and to save 30 games as a reliever?

Dennis Eckersley of the Oakland Athletics. In 1978, Eckersley won 20 games and lost 8 for the Boston Red Sox. He then went on to become a premier reliever for the Athletics. From 1988–1991, Eckersley posted 45, 33, 48, and 43 saves.

Who were "the Whiz Kids"?

The 1950 Philadelphia
Phillies had so many
young players on its pen-
nant-winning team that
they received the nick-
name—"the Whiz Kids."
Some of the young play-
ers on that team were:

Robin Roberts, pitcher—23 years old
Curt Simmons, pitcher—21 years old
Granny Hamner, shortstop—23 years old
Willie Jones, third base—24 years old
Del Ennis, outfield—25 years old
Richie Ashburn, outfield—23 years old

Walter Alston managed the Brooklyn and Los Angeles Dodgers for 23 seasons, but did he ever play in any major league games?

Yes. On September 27, 1936, he appeared in
one game for the St. Louis Cardinals when he
was sent in as a late-inning substitute for
Johnny Mize. In his only major league game,
the future manager made one error in two
chances and, in his only major league at bat,
struck out.

How many brother shortstop/second basemen combinations have there been in the major leagues?

There have been five such brother combinations. They are:

1. Lou and Dino Chiozza of the 1935 Philadelphia Phillies.
2. Granny and Garvin Hamner of the 1945 Philadelphia Phillies.
3. Milt and Frank Bolling of the 1958 Detroit Tigers.
4. Eddie and Johnny O'Brien of the Pittsburgh Pirates (mid 1950s).
5. Cal and Billy Ripken of the 1987 Baltimore Orioles.

Who was the first major-leaguer to hit 30 home runs and steal at least 30 bases in the same season?

The first member of the 30–30 club was Ken Williams of the St. Louis Browns. In 1922, he hit 39 homers and stole 37 bases. It took 34 years for another player to accomplish that feat—when Willie Mays did it for the San Francisco Giants in 1956.

Who was the first person to be hired as a full-time statistician by a major league baseball club?

Alan Roth, who was a pioneer in convincing teams to use statistics as a way of creating tactics and stategies. In 1947, he was hired by Branch Rickey, president of the Brooklyn Dodgers, to chart pitches and to provide the Dodger manager with pertinent statistics. Mr. Roth did all the calculations in his head or by using a simple calculator. Today, of course, every major league club uses thousands of statistics provided to them by the magic of computers.

Who was the youngest person to play major league baseball?

Joe Nuxhall (1928–). On June 10, 1944, he was 15 years, 10 months, and 11 days old when he pitched his first game in the major leagues! He became, in fact, the youngest player in the twentieth century ever to play in the major leagues. It is a record that is yet to be broken.

He was signed, while he was still in high school, by the Cincinnati Reds. Unfortunately his first major league appearance was far from a happy one. He came in to pitch the ninth inning, and gave up 5 runs, on 2 hits and 5 walks.

Who was "Fat Freddy"?

Freddie Fitzsimmons, a knuckle-ball pitcher
with the New York Giants and the Brooklyn
Dodgers, stood 5 feet 11 inches and weighed
200 pounds. In spite of his unflattering nickname, he compiled an impressive record—217
victories against 146 defeats, and he pitched in
three World Series—two with the Giants and
one with the Dodgers.

Although Pete Gray hit only .218 for the lowly St. Louis Browns in 1945, why is he one of the more memorable major-leaguers to have ever played the game?

Before coming up to the St. Louis Browns, Pete Gray played for the Memphis Chicks in the Southern Association. In 1944, Pete Gray hit .333 and stole 68 bases. That year he was voted the most valuable player in his league—and yet, he had only one arm! Gray had lost his right arm in a boyhood accident, but he was able to overcome his handicap and play baseball at the minor and major league levels. As an outfielder, he was graceful. He would catch the ball, quickly stuff his mitt under the stump of his right arm, and then fire the ball into the infield.

Who was known as "the Count"?

John Montefusco, who played in the major leagues from 1974 to 1986, pitching for the San Francisco Giants, the Atlanta Braves, the San Diego Padres, and the New York Yankees, received that sobriquet because his last name reminded fans and fellow players of that great novel—*The Count of Monte Cristo* by Alexander Dumas.

What great feat did "Half-Pint" Rye accomplish?

In 1930, Gene Rye, nicknamed "Half-Pint" (because of his short stature—he stood only 5 feet 6 inches—and because of the reference to the alcoholic beverage rye), played outfield for the Waco Cubs in the Texas League. In the eighth inning of a game against San Antonio, he hit 3 home runs in a single inning! Waco scored 18 runs in that inning and Rye batted in 8 of them. The following year, Half-Pint Rye was called up to the big leagues by the Boston Red Sox. That season he came to bat 39 times, but batted only .179 with no home runs. It was his only season in the major leagues.

Who was the major-leaguer to win both the Rookie of the Year and the Most Valuable Player awards in the same season?

Fred Lynn of the 1975 Red Sox. He also was a Gold Glove winner that year and *The Sporting News* Player of the Year.

That year Lynn batted .331, hit 47 doubles (to set a record for rookies), and hit 21 homers. He batted in 105 runs. His slugging average of .566 was also the highest ever for a rookie.

How did Fred Merkle receive the unflattering nickname of "bonehead"?

In spite of the fact that Fred Merkle was a pretty decent ballplayer, he is remembered mostly for a mistake he made on September 23, 1908—a mental lapse that cost his team the pennant. On an apparent game-winning hit in an important game against the Chicago Cubs, Fred Merkle did not step on second base. The Cubs retrieved the ball and stepped on second and Merkle was called out. In spite of the fact that jubilant Giant fans had already spilled onto the field, the game was called a tie. After the teams finished in a tie for the pennant, a replay of the game was won (and hence the pennant) by the Chicago Cubs.

What famous pitcher and broadcaster made famous the phrase, "It's great to be young and a Yankee"?

Waite Hoyt, who was only fifteen years old when he signed his first major league contract with the New York Giants in 1918. He also played for the New York Yankees from 1921–1930.

Who was the youngest person to manage a major league team?

The honors must go to Lou Boudreau. He was all of 24 when he became manager of the Cleveland Indians in 1942. Before Boudreau there was Bucky (Stanley Raymond) Harris. In 1924, at the grand old age of 28, he became the manager of the Washington Senators. (No wonder Bucky was referred to by the press as "the Boy Wonder"!) In any case, becoming a manager of a major league team, before the age of 30, is quite an accomplishment.

Who was the youngest major league player ever to hit a home run?

That honor goes to a Brooklyn Dodgers shortstop named Tommy Brown. On August 20, 1945, Brown hit a home run off Preacher Roe of the Pittsburgh Pirates. At the time, Brown was only 17 years and 8 months old.

Tommy Brown played for 9 years in the majors and compiled a .241 batting average, with 31 homers and 159 RBI's in 494 games. His nickname was "Buckshot."

Who was Eddie Gaedel?

Eddie Gaedel was a three foot, seven inch midget who, in 1951, was used as a pinch hitter in a game between the St. Louis Browns and the Detroit Tigers. Against Tiger pitcher Bob Cain, Gaedel, because of the very short strike zone from his shoulders to his knees, walked on four straight high pitches and trotted to first base, where he was removed for a runner. It was Eddie Gaedel's only major league at bat.

How many brothers and sisters did Detroit baseball star Willie Watterson Horton have?

Willie Horton, who was the comeback player of the year in 1979 and slugged 325 homers in his career, was the youngest of 21 children.

Was Pete Gray the only player with one arm to play in the major leagues?

Pete Gray was the only one-armed player in the twentieth century, but back in the 1880s there was a pitcher named Hugh Ignatius Daily (sometimes spelled Daly). He pitched from 1882 through 1887 for such National League teams as Buffalo, Cleveland, St. Louis, and Washington, D.C., and won 73 games while losing 89. He was called "One Arm Daily" because he had no left arm. On September 13, 1883, One Arm Daily pitched a no-hitter against Philadelphia.

In 1884, he struck out 483 batters and led the National League in strike-outs.

ONE, TWO, THREE STRIKES YOU'RE OUT!

Statistics You May or May Not Have Known About Baseball

How many baseball teams have hit 225 or more home runs in a season?

Only three. The 1961 New York Yankees, with Roger Maris (61 homers) and Mickey Mantle (54 homers), led the way with 240 homers to set the single-season record. The runners-up are the 1963 Minnesota Twins and the 1987 Detroit Tigers, both with 225 homers.

Has any first-year player ever batted over .300 and also hit 30 or more home runs and batted in at least 100 runs?

Yes. Six rookies, in fact, have been able to accomplish that feat:

Year	Player	Team	Avg.	HR	RBI
1993	Mike Piazza	Dodgers	.318	35	112
1950	Walt Dropo	Red Sox	.322	34	144
1939	Ted Williams	Red Sox	.327	31	145
1937	Rudy York	Tigers	.307	35	142
1934	Hal Trosky	Indians	.330	35	142
1930	Wally Berger	Braves	.310	38	119

How many pitchers have won more than 400 games in their careers?

Only two—Cy Young (511 victories) and Walter Johnson (416 victories).

Who holds the major league record for hitting the most grand slams in a season?

Don Mattingly of the New York Yankees. In 1987, Mattingly hit 6 grand slam home runs to set the record.

How many teams in major league history led their leagues from opening day until the day they clinched the pennant?

Only four teams have managed the feat of staying in first place for every day of a season. They were: the 1984 Detroit Tigers, the 1955 Brooklyn Dodgers, the 1927 New York Yankees, and the 1923 New York Giants.

Have any players played all nine positions in a major league game?

Yes. On September 22, 1968, Cesar Tovar of the Minnesota Twins played a different position in each inning. Bert Campaneris of the Oakland Athletics also accomplished the feat.

How many players have hit more than 15 pinch-hit homers in their careers?

Only 5 major-leaguers have accomplished that feat. They are:

Cliff Johnson—20
Jerry Lynch—18
Smoky Burgess—16
William J. Brown—16
Willie McCovey—16

What is the most number of runs scored by one player in a single inning?

The major league record is 3 runs in one inning. The feat was accomplished twice before the 1900s, but only Sammy White, catcher for the Boston Red Sox, accomplished that feat in the twentieth century. White scored 3 runs in the seventh inning on June 18, 1953.

What designated hitter achieved the highest batting average for a single season?

That honor goes to Mike Easler. He hit .313 in 1984, but he played 126 games as a designated hitter, and in those games hit .330.

How many players in major league history have ever made unassisted triple plays, and who was the last player to accomplish that feat?

Only 11 players have ever made unassisted triple plays. The last player to accomplish that feat was John Valentin, shortstop for the Boston Red Sox. On Friday night, July 8, 1994, Valentin caught a hard liner from the bat of Seattle's designated hitter Marc Newfield. The two runners on base had been going with the pitch, so Valentin stepped on second and tagged the runner (Keith Mitchell) coming in from first.

Before Valentin, the last major-leaguer to turn in an unassisted triple play had been Philadelphia second baseman Mickey Morandini who did it on September 20, 1992. "It really happened so fast, it didn't hit me until I got into the dugout," Morandini said. "Then I realized I'd done something few people have done."

Other players who have turned in unassisted triple plays have been:

Ron Hanson—Washington shortstop—July 30, 1968

Johnny Neun—Detroit first baseman—May 31, 1927

Jim Cooney—Chicago Cubs shortstop—May 30, 1927

Glenn Wright—Pittsburgh shortstop—May 7, 1925

Ernie Padgett—Boston Braves shortstop—October 6, 1923

George Burns—Boston Red Sox first baseman—September 14, 1923

Bill Wambsganss—Cleveland second baseman—October 10, 1920

Neal Ball—Cleveland shortstop—July 19, 1909

Paul Hines—Providence outfielder—May 8, 1878

All the triple plays in the twentieth century have come with runners on first and second. Bill Wambsganss's triple play occurred in the 1920 World Series against the Brooklyn Dodgers.

What is the most number of innings played in one major league game?

Twenty-six innings. On May 1, 1920, the Brooklyn Dodgers played the Boston Braves for 26 innings. The game ended in a 1–1 tie.

How many pitchers have pitched more than 500 complete games?

Only a half-dozen pitchers have accomplished that feat. They are:

Cy Young—751
James F. Galvin—641
Tim Keefe—554
Walter Johnson—531
Charles A. Nichols—531
Mickey Welch—525

All of those great pitchers played in the days before relief pitching was raised to the art it is now. In modern baseball, with its emphasis upon middle relievers and closers, complete games get more and more rare. The 1991 New York Yankees, for example, went over 75 consecutive games without one of their pitchers getting a complete game victory.

What is the most times a player has come to bat in a nine-inning game?

Would you believe 8 times? Since 1900, nine players have accomplished that feat. The last major-leaguer to face a pitcher 8 times in a nine-inning game was Clyde F. Vollmer of the Boston Red Sox on June 8, 1950.

Has any major-leaguer ever struck out 100 times in a season without hitting a single home run?

Just one. The first player in any league to strike out 100 times without hitting a home run was the Toronto Blue Jays shortstop Manuel Lee, who accomplished this dubious feat during the 1991 season.

What major-leaguer played in more games than any other?

That record is held by Pete Rose, who, from 1963–1986, played in 3,562 games for the Cincinnati Reds, the Philadelphia Phillies, and the Montreal Expos.

The American League record for most games played is held by Carl Yastrzemski, who played 3,308 games (1961–1983)—all for one team, the Boston Red Sox.

When Babe Ruth became the all-time major league home-run leader in 1921, whose record did he surpass?

The home run record holder at that time was a National League player named Roger Connor who had amassed 136 career home runs.

How many players ever played for two different major league clubs on the very same day?

It has sometimes happened that a team, while playing a doubleheader, has traded or sold players between games. So far, three players hold the distinction of playing for two teams on the same day. They are:

1. Max Flack. On May 30, 1922, as part of a day/night contest, Flack played for the Chicago Cubs in the first game and then for the St. Louis Cardinals in the second game.
2. Clifton E. Heathcote (who was traded for Flack) played the first game for the Cardinals and the night game for the Cubs.
3. Joel R. Youngblood. On August 4, 1982, Youngblood played the first game of a doubleheader for the New York Mets and the second game for the Montreal Expos.

Who holds the record for the number of bases stolen in a single inning?

Josh Devore of the old New York Giants. On June 20, 1912, the Giants played the Boston Braves. In the ninth inning of that game, DeVore reached first base safely. He stole second, then stole third. The Giants kept on batting around. DeVore came to bat again. Again he reached first, stole second, then stole third.

He stole four bases in a single inning!

Since 1920 has any major-leaguer played at least 10 seasons and never had a batting average below .300 in his career?

It would seem that quite a few players would have been able to accomplish that feat, and yet, as strange as it sounds, only one major leaguer (as of 1994) has been able to play out his entire career (at least 10 full seasons) and not bat lower than .300. The player that accomplished that feat is four-time National League batting champion Tony Gwynn. In 1990, Gwynn hit .309—so far the lowest batting average of his career.

What Hall of Famer hit into more double plays than any other player?

Hank Aaron. During his great career, he grounded into 328 double plays—305 while he was in the National League, 23 in the American League.

Has any player ever gotten more than 6 hits in a nine-inning game?

Yes. On September 16, 1975, the Pittsburgh Pirates defeated the Chicago Cubs at Wrigley Field by the lopsided score of 22–0. In that nine-inning game, Rennie Stennett made 7 hits. Stennett's 7 hits are actually more hits than any National League player has ever achieved in even an extra-inning game. The 22–0 score is the most one-sided shutout in major league play since 1900.

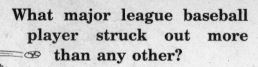

What major league baseball player struck out more than any other?

Reggie Jackson. He struck out 2,247 times in 8,649 at bats. No other player has struck out more than 2,000 times.

Have any major league players achieved 2,000 hits in their careers, *and* hit 300 home runs, *and* stole 300 or more bases?

Yes. Only two players have accomplished that feat—Willie Mays and Andre Dawson.

What is the record for the most hits allowed by a pitcher in a nine-inning game?

Would you believe 26 hits? On September 11, 1936, Horace Milton Lisenbee who was pitching for the Philadelphia Athletics, gave up 26 hits. Lisenbee finished that year with a dismal record—one win and seven losses with a 6.20 earned run average. Certainly that day in September did not help him any.

When a baseball bat hits a baseball, how long are the bat and ball actually in contact with one another?

About one-one thousandth of a second, according to Robert K. Adair, Sterling Professor of Physics at Yale University and author of *The Physics of Baseball*.

What is the major league record for the number of players with 20 or more home runs on a single team in a season?

The most players with 20 or more home runs on a team in a season is six. The record is shared by a number of teams. The 1961 Yankees had Roger Maris (61 homers), Mickey Mantle (54), Bill Skowron (28), Yogi Berra (22), Elston Howard (21), and Johnny Blanchard (21).

The 1964 Minnesota Twins had Harmon Killebrew (49 homers), Tony Oliva (32), Bob Allison (32), Jimmie Hall (25), Don Mincher (23), and Zoilo Versalles (20).

The 1965 Milwaukee Braves had Hank Aaron (32 homers), Eddie Mathews (32), Mack Jones (31), Joe Torre (27), Felipe Alou (23), and Gene Oliver (21).

In 1986, the Detroit Tigers also had six 20-or-more homer players: Darrel Evans (29 homers), Kirk Gibson (28), Lance Parrish (22), Alan Trammell (21), Lou Whitaker (20), and Darnell Coles (20).

Is it possible for an infielder to be credited with 27 put-outs in a nine-inning game without ever once touching the ball?

It is possible, but highly unlikely. Here is how it could happen: The pitcher walks a batter. The next batter hits a grounder and the baseball hits the runner. The runner is out and the nearest infielder is credited with a put-out. If this happened 27 times in a game, with the same infielder involved, well . . .

What pitchers hold the record for the most strike-outs in a single game?

In the history of the major leagues, there has been only one player who has struck out 20 batters in a game, and that was Roger Clemens of the Boston Red Sox in a game against the Seattle Mariners on April 29, 1986.

Pitchers who have struck out 19 batters in a game are:

David Cone, New York Mets vs. Philadelphia Phillies (October 6, 1991)
Nolan Ryan, California Angels vs. Boston Red Sox (August 12, 1974)
Tom Seaver, New York Mets vs. San Diego Padres (April 22, 1970)

How many times has the World Series been decided by a hit in the final at bat?

As of the 1993 World Series, only seven times has the series been decided in the final at bat.

In 1924, the Washington (D.C.) Senators battled the New York Giants into the seventh game, and that game went into extra innings. In the twelfth inning, the score was 3–3, and Earl McNeely of the Senators singled home Muddy Ruel from second base. Jack Bentley of the Giants was the losing pitcher.

Five years later, the 1929 series went only five games, but that series, too, was decided in the final at bat. Bing Miller of the Philadelphia Athletics doubled off Pat Malone of the Chicago Cubs, driving in Al Simmons from second with the go-ahead run. The Athletics won the game 3–2.

In 1935, the Detroit Tigers faced the Chicago Cubs in the Series. In the sixth game, with the score tied 3–3, Goose Goslin's single in the bottom of the ninth brought in Mickey Cochrane from second and the Tigers won. Cubs pitcher Larry French was the losing pitcher that day.

In 1953, those arch rivals, the New York Yankees and the Brooklyn Dodgers, squared off.

The Yankees entered the sixth game, leading the series, three games to two. In the bottom of the ninth, with the score tied 3–3, and with Brooklyn's Clem Labine on the mound and Hank Bauer of the Yankees on second, Billy Martin singled and the Yankees took the series.

The 1960 World Series between the Pittsburgh Pirates and the Yankees went the full seven games. In the ninth inning, with the score tied 9–9, Bill Mazeroski led off the bottom of the ninth for the Pirates and struck a home run off Ralph Terry. It was not quite "the blast heard 'round the world," but it was heard far and wide.

The 1991 series between the Minnesota Twins and the Atlanta Braves was won by the Twins 1–0 in the tenth inning of the seventh game when Gene Larkin singled off Alejandro Peña, scoring Dan Gladden from third base.

And last, but not least, the Toronto Blue Jays, on Joe Carter's three-run homer off Mitch "Wild Thing" Williams, beat the Philadelphia Phillies 8–6 and gave the Jays the series in six games.

These late-inning heroics are the stuff of baseball dreams.

What is the longest number of innings that any major league relief pitcher has ever pitched?

On June 17, 1915, George "Zip" Zabel of the Chicago Cubs was called into the game in the first inning, with 2 outs, against the Brooklyn Dodgers. By the time the smoke had cleared, Zip won the game 4–3 in the nineteenth inning! That's the longest relief effort on the books. By the end of that game, Zip probably didn't have much zip left.

Have any major league hitters hit 20 doubles, triples, and homers in a single season?

So far 6 players have accomplished that feat:

Player	Team	Year	2B	3B	HR	Avg.
Buck Freeman	Washington Nationals	1899	20	26	25	.318
Wildfire Schulte	Chicago Cubs	1911	30	21	21	.300
Jim Bottomley	St. Louis Cardinals	1928	42	20	31	.325
Jeff Heath	Cleveland Indians	1941	32	20	24	.340
Willie Mays	New York Giants	1957	26	20	35	.333
George Brett	Kansas City Royals	1979	42	20	23	.329

What is the most number of home runs ever hit by a single team in one game?

On September 14, 1987, the Toronto Blue Jays clubbed 10 home runs against the Baltimore Orioles. That's a major league record!

There have been numerous outstanding outfields in major league history, but what was the best hitting outfield of all time?

Many historians of the game would give the nod to the 1894 Philadelphia Athletics as being the best hitting outfield of all time. The outfield consisted of Sam Thompson, who hit .404, Ed Delahanty, who hit .400, and Billy Hamilton, who only managed a batting average of .399. The three outfielders had a combined batting average of .400.

How many major league pitchers have won at least 100 games in both the American and National leagues?

So far, only 7 pitchers have accomplished that feat. They are:

Dennis Martinez, 108–93 AL (Baltimore), 100–72 NL (Montreal)

Nolan Ryan, 189–160 AL (California, Texas) 135–132 NL (Mets, Houston)

Ferguson Jenkins, 115–93 AL (Texas, Boston), 169–133 NL (Philadelphia, Chicago)

Gaylord Perry, 139–130 AL (Cleveland, Texas, Yankees, Seattle, Kansas City), 175–135 NL (San Francisco, San Diego, Atlanta)

Jim Bunning, 118–107 AL (Detroit), 106–97 NL (Philadelphia, Pittsburgh, Los Angeles)

Al Orth, 104–117 AL (Washington, New York), 100–72 NL (Philadelphia)

Cy Young, 221–141 AL (Boston, Cleveland), 290–175 NL (Cleveland, St. Louis, Boston)

What is the most number of strike-outs recorded by a pitcher in a losing effort?

The record in a losing effort was set by Steve Carlton of the St. Louis Cardinals when he struck out 19 New York Mets batters (on September 15, 1969) and still lost 4–3.

Has any team ever had a winning percentage of .500 or better and still finished in last place?

The California Angels in 1991 had a won-lost percentage of .500 and still finished last in their division. The complete standings for the American League West that year were:

Team	Wins	Losses	Pct.	Games Back
Minnesota	95	67	.586	-
Chicago	87	75	.537	8
Texas	85	77	.525	10
Oakland	84	78	.519	11
Seattle	83	79	.512	12
Kansas City	82	80	.506	13
California	81	81	.500	14

What is the most number of runs scored by a team in two consecutive games?

Forty-nine runs! On June 7, 1950, the Boston Red Sox played the St. Louis Browns and won by the score of 20–4. On the following day, the Red Sox did even better, defeating the Browns 29–4.

Did New York Yankee home run star Mickey Mantle hit more career home runs at Yankee Stadium or on the road?

Mantle hit more homers on the road. Of his 536 homers, 266 were at home and 270 were hit in other ballparks.

Has any player ever hit 50 or more home runs for a last-place ball club?

Yes, but it has happened only once. In 1947, Ralph Kiner slugged 51 homers, but his team—the Pittsburgh Pirates—won only 62 games that year (they lost 92 games) and finished dead last.

How many players have hit 4 home runs in a single game?

Four homers in one game is the record every slugger envies. The feat has been accomplished only twelve times. The players who did it are:

Robert L. Lowe, Boston, NL (May 30, 1894)

Edward J. Delahanty, Philadelphia, NL (July 13, 1896)

Charles H. Klein, Philadelphia, NL (July 10, 1936—10 innings)

Gil Hodges, Brooklyn, NL (August 31, 1950)

Joe Adcock, Milwaukee, NL (July 31, 1954)

Willie Mays, San Francisco, NL (April 30, 1961)

Mike Schmidt, Philadelphia, NL (April 17, 1976—10 innings)

J. Robert Horner, Atlanta, NL (July 6, 1986)

Mark Whitten, St. Louis, NL (September 7, 1993)

Lou Gehrig, New York, AL (June 3, 1932)

J. Patrick Seerey, Chicago, AL (July 18, 1948—11 innings)

Rocky Colavito, Cleveland, AL (June 10, 1959)

Have any major league batters ever driven in 10 or more runs in a single game?

Yes. Nine players have accomplished that feat. Two players, in fact, have knocked in a dozen runs in a game. Players who have driven in 10 or more runs in one game are:

Mark Whitten—12 RBIs, Cardinals, September 7, 1993

Jim Bottomley—12 RBIs, Cardinals, September 16, 1924

Tony Lazzeri—11 RBIs, Yankees, May 24, 1936

Phil Weintraub—11 RBIs, Giants, April 30, 1944

Walker Cooper—10 RBIs, Reds, July 6, 1949

Rudy York—10 RBIs, Red Sox, July 27, 1946

Norm Zauchin—10 RBIs, Red Sox, May 27, 1955

Reggie Jackson—10 RBIs, Oakland Athletics, July 14, 1969

Fred Lynn—10 RBIs, Red Sox, June 18, 1975

Is it true that Shoeless Joe Jackson used a bat that weighed 3 pounds?

As improbable as it seems, it is true that the great Shoeless Joe Jackson (who is one of the old baseball stars portrayed in the movie *Field of Dreams*) swung a bat that weighed 48 ounces. He didn't do so badly with it either. Not only is Shoeless Joe the only player to hit over .400 in his rookie year (he hit .408 in 1911); he finished his career with a lifetime batting average of .356.

Babe Ruth, on the other hand, swung a bat that weighed between 37 and 47 ounces, while Jimmy Foxx's bat weighed in at 44 ounces. Ted Williams used a bat in the 32–34 ounce range, as did Mickey Mantle. Contemporary players such as Frank Thomas and Juan Gonzalez tend to use lighter bats because today's pitchers throw hard sliders.

Has any baseball pitcher ever pitched a no-hitter in his very first major league game?

Yes, only one. The pitcher to accomplish that feat was none other than Alva L. "Bobo" Hollomon of the St. Louis Browns. On May 16, 1953, Hollomon started his very first major league game against the Philadelphia Athletics. He gave up no hits, and the Browns defeated the Athletics 6–0. Strangely enough, that game turned out to be the only complete game that Hollomon ever pitched in the majors!

What team compiled the worst won-and-lost record in the history of major league baseball?

That dubious honor must go to the Cleveland Spiders of the National League in 1899. During that season, the Spiders won only 20 games and lost 134.

Other teams who suffered through miserable seasons were the 1916 Philadelphia Athletics who won 36 and lost 117, and the 1935 Boston Braves, who won 38 and lost 115.

What is the most runs scored by one team in a single game?

On June 8, 1950, the Boston Red Sox had one great day at the ballpark. Not only did the Red Sox pound out 28 hits to beat the St. Louis Browns 29–4, the team set all kinds of records in the process: 29 runs is the most ever scored by a team; the most long hits in a game—17 (9 doubles, 1 triple, and 7 homers); most total bases—60; most extra bases on long hits—32.

What catcher caught more no-hit games (entire games) than any other?

Raymond W. Schalk of the Chicago White Sox. He caught 4 no-hitters in his seventeen-year (1912–1928) career. He caught 2 no-hitters in 1914, one in 1917, and the last in 1922. Schalk also holds the all-time record for catchers making double plays—217.

What must be the speed of a bat to hit an 85-mph fastball 400 feet to dead center field under standard conditions (that is, moderate temperature and no wind)?

Again according to Dr. Robert K. Adair, author of *The Physics of Baseball*, the bat speed required to hit a baseball 400 feet is about 76 miles per hour. To hit the ball 450 feet, the bat must be swung at a velocity of 86 miles per hour.

WORLD SERIES RESULTS

Year	Winner	League	Loser	League	Games
1903	Boston Red Sox	AL	Pittsburgh Pirates	NL	5–3
1904	No series	—	—	—	—
1905	New York Giants	NL	Philadelphia Athletics	AL	4–1
1906	Chicago White Sox	AL	Chicago Cubs	NL	4–2
1907	Chicago Cubs	NL	Detroit Tigers	AL	4–0
1908	Chicago Cubs	NL	Detroit Tigers	AL	4–1
1909	Pittsburgh Pirates	NL	Detroit Tigers	AL	4–3
1910	Philadelphia Athletics	AL	Chicago Cubs	NL	4–1
1911	Philadelphia Athletics	AL	New York Giants	NL	4–2
1912	Boston Red Sox	AL	New York Giants	NL	4–3
1913	Philadelphia Athletics	AL	New York Giants	NL	4–1
1914	Boston Braves	NL	Philadelphia Athletics	AL	4–0
1915	Boston Red Sox	AL	Philadelphia Phillies	NL	4–1
1916	Boston Red Sox	AL	Brooklyn Dodgers	NL	4–1
1917	Chicago White Sox	AL	New York Giants	NL	4–2
1918	Boston Red Sox	AL	Chicago Cubs	NL	4–2
1919	Cincinnati Reds	NL	Chicago White Sox	AL	5–3
1920	Cleveland Indians	AL	Brooklyn Dodgers	NL	5–2
1921	New York Giants	NL	New York Yankees	AL	5–3
1922	New York Giants	NL	New York Yankees	AL	4–0
1923	New York Yankees	AL	New York Giants	NL	4–2

Year	Winner	League	Loser	League	Games
1924	Washington Senators	AL	New York Giants	NL	4–3
1925	Pittsburgh Pirates	NL	Washington Senators	AL	4–3
1926	St. Louis Cardinals	NL	New York Yankees	AL	4–3
1927	New York Yankees	AL	Pittsburgh Pirates	NL	4–0
1928	New York Yankees	AL	St. Louis Cardinals	NL	4–0
1929	Philadelphia Athletics	AL	Chicago Cubs	NL	4–1
1930	Philadelphia Athletics	AL	St. Louis Cardinals	NL	4–2
1931	St. Louis Cardinals	NL	Philadelphia Athletics	AL	4–3
1932	New York Yankees	AL	Chicago Cubs	NL	4–0
1933	New York Giants	NL	Washington Senators	AL	4–1
1934	St. Louis Cardinals	NL	Detroit Tigers	AL	4–3
1935	Detroit Tigers	AL	Chicago Cubs	NL	4–2
1936	New York Yankees	AL	New York Giants	NL	4–2
1937	New York Yankees	AL	New York Giants	NL	4–1
1938	New York Yankees	AL	Chicago Cubs	NL	4–0
1939	New York Yankees	AL	Cincinnati Reds	NL	4–0
1940	Cincinnati Reds	NL	Detroit Tigers	AL	4–3
1941	New York Yankees	AL	Brooklyn Dodgers	NL	4–1
1942	St. Louis Cardinals	NL	New York Yankees	AL	4–1
1943	New York Yankees	AL	St. Louis Cardinals	NL	4–1
1944	St. Louis Cardinals	NL	St. Louis Browns	AL	4–2
1945	Detroit Tigers	AL	Chicago Cubs	NL	4–3
1946	St. Louis Cardinals	NL	Boston Red Sox	AL	4–3
1947	New York Yankees	AL	Brooklyn Dodgers	NL	4–3

WORLD SERIES RESULTS (*continued*)

Year	Winner	League	Loser	League	Games
1948	Cleveland Indians	AL	Boston Braves	NL	4-2
1949	New York Yankees	AL	Brooklyn Dodgers	NL	4-1
1950	New York Yankees	AL	Philadelphia Phillies	NL	4-0
1951	New York Yankees	AL	New York Giants	NL	4-2
1952	New York Yankees	AL	Brooklyn Dodgers	NL	4-3
1953	New York Yankees	AL	Brooklyn Dodgers	NL	4-2
1954	New York Giants	NL	Cleveland Indians	AL	4-0
1955	Brooklyn Dodgers	NL	New York Yankees	AL	4-3
1956	New York Yankees	AL	Brooklyn Dodgers	NL	4-3
1957	Milwaukee Braves	NL	New York Yankees	AL	4-3
1958	New York Yankees	AL	Milwaukee Braves	NL	4-3
1959	Los Angeles Dodgers	NL	Chicago White Sox	AL	4-2
1960	Pittsburgh Pirates	NL	New York Yankees	AL	4-3
1961	New York Yankees	AL	Cincinnati Reds	NL	4-1
1962	New York Yankees	AL	San Francisco Giants	NL	4-3
1963	Los Angeles Dodgers	NL	New York Yankees	AL	4-0
1964	St. Louis Cardinals	NL	New York Yankees	AL	4-3
1965	Los Angeles Dodgers	NL	Minnesota Twins	AL	4-3
1966	Baltimore Orioles	AL	Los Angeles Dodgers	NL	4-0
1967	St. Louis Cardinals	NL	Boston Red Sox	AL	4-3
1968	Detroit Tigers	AL	St. Louis Cardinals	NL	4-3
1969	New York Mets	NL	Baltimore Orioles	AL	4-1

Year	Winner	League	Loser	League	Games
1970	Baltimore Orioles	AL	Cincinnati Reds	NL	4–1
1971	Pittsburgh Pirates	NL	Baltimore Orioles	AL	4–3
1972	Oakland Athletics	AL	Cincinnati Reds	NL	4–3
1973	Oakland Athletics	AL	New York Mets	NL	4–3
1974	Oakland Athletics	AL	Los Angeles Dodgers	NL	4–1
1975	Cincinnati Reds	NL	Boston Red Sox	AL	4–3
1976	Cincinnati Reds	NL	New York Yankees	AL	4–0
1977	New York Yankees	AL	Los Angeles Dodgers	NL	4–2
1978	New York Yankees	AL	Los Angeles Dodgers	NL	4–2
1979	Pittsburgh Pirates	NL	Baltimore Orioles	AL	4–3
1980	Philadelphia Phillies	NL	Kansas City Royals	AL	4–2
1981	Los Angeles Dodgers	NL	New York Yankees	AL	4–2
1982	St. Louis Cardinals	NL	Milwaukee Brewers	AL	4–3
1983	Baltimore Orioles	AL	Philadelphia Phillies	NL	4–1
1984	Detroit Tigers	AL	San Diego Padres	NL	4–1
1985	Kansas City Royals	AL	St. Louis Cardinals	NL	4–3
1986	New York Mets	NL	Boston Red Sox	AL	4–3
1987	Minnesota Twins	AL	St. Louis Cardinals	NL	4–3
1988	Los Angeles Dodgers	NL	Oakland Athletics	AL	4–1
1989	Oakland Athletics	AL	San Francisco Giants	NL	4–2
1990	Cincinnati Reds	NL	Oakland Athletics	AL	4–0
1991	Minnesota Twins	AL	Atlanta Braves	NL	4–2
1992	Toronto Blue Jays	AL	Atlanta Braves	NL	4–2
1993	Toronto Blue Jays	AL	Philadelphia Phillies	NL	4–2
1994	World series cancelled because of strike by players				

MOST VALUABLE PLAYER SELECTIONS
(selected by the Baseball Writers Association)

American League

Lefty Grove
Philadelphia, 1931

Jimmy Foxx
Philadelphia, 1932–33

Mickey Cochrane
Detroit, 1934

Hank Greenberg
Detroit, 1935

Lou Gehrig
New York, 1936

Charlie Gehringer
Detroit, 1937

Jimmy Foxx
Boston, 1938

Joe DiMaggio
New York, 1939

Hank Greenberg
Detroit, 1940

Joe DiMaggio
New York, 1941

Joe Gordon
New York, 1942

Spurgeon Chandler
New York, 1943

Hal Newhouser
Detroit, 1944–45

Ted Williams
Boston, 1946

Joe DiMaggio
New York, 1947

Lou Boudreau
Cleveland, 1948

Ted Williams
Boston, 1949

Phil Rizzuto
New York, 1950

Yogi Berra
New York, 1951

Bobby Shantz
Philadelphia, 1952

Al Rosen
Cleveland, 1953

Yogi Berra
New York, 1954–55

Mickey Mantle
New York, 1956–57

Jackie Jensen
Boston, 1958

Nellie Fox
Chicago, 1959

Roger Maris
New York, 1960–61

Mickey Mantle
New York, 1962

Elston Howard
New York, 1963

Brooks Robinson
Baltimore, 1964

Zoilo Versalles
Minnesota, 1965

Frank Robinson
Baltimore, 1966

Carl Yastrzemski
Boston, 1967

Dennis McLain
Detroit, 1968

Harmon Killebrew
Minnesota, 1969

John (Boog) Powell
Baltimore, 1970
Vida Blue
Oakland, 1971
Dick Allen
Chicago, 1972
Reggie Jackson
Oakland, 1973
Jeff Burroughs
Texas, 1974
Fred Lynn
Boston, 1975
Thurman Munson
New York, 1976
Rod Carew
Minnesota, 1977
Jim Rice
Boston, 1978
Don Baylor
California, 1979
George Brett
Kansas City, 1980
Rollie Fingers
Milwaukee, 1981
Robin Yount
Milwaukee, 1982

Cal Ripken, Jr.
Baltimore, 1983
Willie Hernandez
Detroit, 1984
Don Mattingly
New York, 1985
Roger Clemens
Boston, 1986
George Bell
Toronto, 1987
Jose Canseco
Oakland, 1988
Robin Yount
Milwaukee, 1989
Rickey Henderson
Oakland, 1990
Cal Ripken, Jr.
Baltimore, 1991
Dennis Eckersley
Oakland, 1992
Frank Thomas
Chicago, 1993
Frank Thomas
Chicago, 1994

National League

Frank Frisch
St. Louis, 1931
Chuck Klein
Philadelphia, 1932
Carl Hubbell
New York, 1933
Dizzy Dean
St. Louis, 1934
Gabby Hartnett
Chicago, 1935

Carl Hubbell
New York, 1936
Joe Medwick
St. Louis, 1937
Ernie Lombardi
Cincinnati, 1938
Bucky Walters
Cincinnati, 1939
Frank McCormick
Cincinnati, 1940

Dolph Camilli
Brooklyn, 1941
Mort Cooper
St. Louis, 1942
Stan Musial
St. Louis, 1943
Marty Marion
St. Louis, 1944
Phil Cavarretta
Chicago, 1945
Stan Musial
St. Louis, 1946
Bob Elliott
Boston, 1947
Stan Musial
St. Louis, 1948
Jackie Robinson
Brooklyn, 1949
Jim Konstanty
Philadelphia, 1950
Roy Campanella
Brooklyn, 1951
Hank Sauer
Chicago, 1952
Roy Campanella
Brooklyn, 1953
Willie Mays
New York, 1954
Roy Campanella
Brooklyn, 1955
Don Newcombe
Brooklyn, 1956
Henry Aaron
Milwaukee, 1957
Ernie Banks
Chicago, 1958–59

Dick Groat
Pittsburgh, 1960
Frank Robinson
Cincinnati, 1961
Maury Wills
Los Angeles, 1962
Sandy Koufax
Los Angeles, 1963
Ken Boyer
St. Louis, 1964
Willie Mays
San Francisco, 1965
Roberto Clemente
Pittsburgh, 1966
Orlando Cepeda
St. Louis, 1967
Bob Gibson
St. Louis, 1968
Willie McCovey
San Francisco, 1969
Johnny Bench
Cincinnati, 1970
Joe Torre
St. Louis, 1971
Johnny Bench
Cincinnati, 1972
Pete Rose
Cincinnati, 1973
Steve Garvey
Los Angeles, 1974
Joe Morgan
Cincinnati, 1975–76
George Foster
Cincinnati, 1977
Dave Parker
Pittsburgh, 1978

Willie Stargell
  Pittsburgh, 1979
Keith Hernandez
  St. Louis, 1979
Mike Schmidt
  Philadelphia, 1980
Mike Schmidt
  Philadelphia, 1981
Dale Murphy
  Atlanta, 1982
Dale Murphy
  Atlanta, 1983
Ryne Sandberg
  Chicago, 1984
Willie McGee
  St. Louis, 1985
Mike Schmidt
  Philadelphia, 1986

Andre Dawson
  Chicago, 1987
Kirk Gibson
  Los Angeles, 1988
Kevin Mitchell
  San Francisco, 1989
Barry Bonds
  Pittsburgh, 1990
Terry Pendleton
  Atlanta, 1991
Barry Bonds
  Pittsburgh, 1992
Barry Bonds
  San Francisco, 1993
Jeff Bagwell
  Houston Astros, 1994

AMERICAN LEAGUE BATTING CHAMPIONS

1901	Nap Lajoie	Philadelphia A's	.422
1902	Ed Delahanty	Washington Senators	.376
1903	Nap Lajoie	Cleveland Indians	.355
1904	Nap Lajoie	Cleveland Indians	.381
1905	Elmer Flick	Cleveland Indians	.306
1906	George Stone	St. Louis Browns	.358
1907	Ty Cobb	Detroit Tigers	.350
1908	Ty Cobb	Detroit Tigers	.324
1909	Ty Cobb	Detroit Tigers	.377
1910	Ty Cobb	Detroit Tigers	.385
1911	Ty Cobb	Detroit Tigers	.420
1912	Ty Cobb	Detroit Tigers	.410
1913	Ty Cobb	Detroit Tigers	.390
1914	Ty Cobb	Detroit Tigers	.368
1915	Ty Cobb	Detroit Tigers	.370
1916	Tris Speaker	Cleveland Indians	.386

AMERICAN LEAGUE BATTING CHAMPIONS
(continued)

1917	Ty Cobb	Detroit Tigers	.383
1918	Ty Cobb	Detroit Tigers	.382
1919	Ty Cobb	Detroit Tigers	.407
1920	George Sisler	St. Louis Browns	.407
1921	Harry Heilmann	Detroit Tigers	.394
1922	George Sisler	St. Louis Browns	.420
1923	Harry Heilmann	Detroit Tigers	.403
1924	Babe Ruth	N.Y. Yankees	.378
1925	Harry Heilmann	Detroit Tigers	.393
1926	Heinie Manush	Detroit Tigers	.377
1927	Harry Heilmann	Detroit Tigers	.398
1928	Goose Goslin	Washington Senators	.379
1929	Lew Fonseca	Cleveland Indians	.369
1930	Al Simmons	Philadelphia A's	.381
1931	Al Simmons	Philadelphia A's	.390
1932	Dale Alexander	Detroit-Boston	.367
1933	Jimmie Foxx	Philadelphia A's	.356
1934	Lou Gehrig	N.Y. Yankees	.363
1935	Buddy Myer	Washington Senators	.349
1936	Luke Appling	Chicago White Sox	.388
1937	Charlie Gehringer	Detroit Tigers	.371
1938	Jimmie Foxx	Boston Red Sox	.349
1939	Joe DiMaggio	N.Y. Yankees	.381
1940	Joe DiMaggio	N.Y. Yankees	.352
1941	Ted Williams	Boston Red Sox	.406
1942	Ted Williams	Boston Red Sox	.356
1943	Luke Appling	Chicago White Sox	.328
1944	Lou Boudreau	Cleveland Indians	.327
1945	Snuffy Stirnweiss	N.Y. Yankees	.309
1946	Mickey Vernon	Washington Senators	.352
1947	Ted Williams	Boston Red Sox	.343
1948	Ted Williams	Boston Red Sox	.369
1949	George Kell	Detroit Tigers	.343
1950	Billy Goodman	Boston Red Sox	.354
1951	Ferris Fain	Philadelphia A's	.344
1952	Ferris Fain	Philadelphia A's	.327

1953	Mickey Vernon	Washington Senators	.337
1954	Bobby Avila	Cleveland Indians	.341
1955	Al Kaline	Detroit Tigers	.340
1956	Mickey Mantle	N.Y. Yankees	.353
1957	Ted Williams	Boston Red Sox	.388
1958	Ted Williams	Boston Red Sox	.328
1959	Harvey Kuenn	Detroit Tigers	.353
1960	Pete Runnels	Boston Red Sox	.320
1961	Norm Cash	Detroit Tigers	.361
1962	Pete Runnels	Boston Red Sox	.326
1963	Carl Yastrzemski	Boston Red Sox	.321
1964	Tony Oliva	Minnesota Twins	.323
1965	Tony Oliva	Minnesota Twins	.321
1966	Frank Robinson	Baltimore Orioles	.316
1967	Carl Yastrzemski	Boston Red Sox	.326
1968	Carl Yastrzemski	Boston Red Sox	.301
1969	Rod Carew	Minnesota Twins	.332
1970	Alex Johnson	California Angels	.329
1971	Tony Oliva	Minnesota Twins	.337
1972	Rod Carew	Minnesota Twins	.318
1973	Rod Carew	Minnesota Twins	.350
1974	Rod Carew	Minnesota Twins	.364
1975	Rod Carew	Minnesota Twins	.359
1976	George Brett	K.C. Royals	.333
1977	Rod Carew	Minnesota Twins	.388
1978	Rod Carew	Minnesota Twins	.333
1979	Fred Lynn	Boston Red Sox	.333
1980	George Brett	K.C. Royals	.390
1981	Carney Lansford	Boston Red Sox	.336
1982	Willie Wilson	K.C. Royals	.332
1983	Wade Boggs	Boston Red Sox	.361
1984	Don Mattingly	N.Y. Yankees	.343
1985	Wade Boggs	Boston Red Sox	.368
1986	Wade Boggs	Boston Red Sox	.357
1987	Wade Boggs	Boston Red Sox	.363
1988	Wade Boggs	Boston Red Sox	.366
1989	Kirby Puckett	Minnesota Twins	.339
1990	George Brett	K.C. Royals	.329

AMERICAN LEAGUE BATTING CHAMPIONS
(continued)

1991	Julio Franco	Texas Rangers	.341
1992	Edgar Martinez	Seattle Mariners	.343
1993	John Olerud	Toronto Blue Jays	.363
1994	Paul O'Neill	N.Y. Yankees	.359

NATIONAL LEAGUE BATTING CHAMPIONS

1876	Roscoe Barnes	Chicago Cubs	.403
1877	James White	Boston Braves	.385
1878	Abner Dalrymple	Milwaukee Brewers	.356
1879	Cap Anson	Chicago Cubs	.407
1880	George Gore	Chicago Cubs	.365
1881	Cap Anson	Chicago Cubs	.399
1882	Dan Brouthers	Buffalo Bisons	.367
1883	Dan Brouthers	Buffalo Bisons	.371
1884	Jim O'Rourke	Buffalo Bisons	.350
1885	Roger Connor	N.Y. Giants	.371
1886	Mike Kelly	Chicago Cubs	.388
1887	Cap Anson	Chicago Cubs	.421
1888	Cap Anson	Chicago Cubs	.343
1889	Dan Brouthers	Boston Braves	.373
1890	Jack Glasscock	N.Y. Giants	.336
1891	Billy Hamilton	Philadelphia Phillies	.338
1892	"Cupid" Childs	Cleveland Spiders	.335
	Dan Brouthers	Brooklyn Dodgers	.335
1893	Hugh Duffy	Boston Braves	.378
1894	Hugh Duffy	Boston Braves	.438
1895	Jesse Burkett	Cleveland Spiders	.423
1896	Jesse Burkett	Cleveland Spiders	.410
1897	Willie Keeler	Baltimore Orioles	.432
1898	Willie Keeler	Baltimore Orioles	.379
1899	Ed Delahanty	Philadelphia Phillies	.408
1900	Honus Wagner	Pittsburgh Pirates	.380
1901	Jesse Burkett	St. Louis Cardinals	.382
1902	C.H. Beaumont	Pittsburgh Pirates	.357
1903	Honus Wagner	Pittsburgh Pirates	.355
1904	Honus Wagner	Pittsburgh Pirates	.349

1905	J. Bentley Seymour	Cincinnati Reds	.377
1906	Honus Wagner	Pittsburgh Pirates	.339
1907	Honus Wagner	Pittsburgh Pirates	.350
1908	Honus Wagner	Pittsburgh Pirates	.354
1909	Honus Wagner	Pittsburgh Pirates	.339
1910	Sherwood Magee	Philadelphia Phillies	.331
1911	Honus Wagner	Pittsburgh Pirates	.334
1912	Heinie Zimmerman	Chicago Cubs	.372
1913	Jake Daubert	Brooklyn Dodgers	.350
1914	Jake Daubert	Brooklyn Dodgers	.329
1915	Larry Doyle	N.Y. Giants	.320
1916	Hal Chase	Cincinnati Reds	.339
1917	Edd Roush	Cincinnati Reds	.341
1918	Zack Wheat	Brooklyn Dodgers	.335
1919	Edd Roush	Cincinnati Reds	.321
1920	Rogers Hornsby	St. Louis Cardinals	.370
1921	Rogers Hornsby	St. Louis Cardinals	.397
1922	Rogers Hornsby	St. Louis Cardinals	.401
1923	Rogers Hornsby	St. Louis Cardinals	.384
1924	Rogers Hornsby	St. Louis Cardinals	.424
1925	Rogers Hornsby	St. Louis Cardinals	.403
1926	Bubbles Hargrave	Cincinnati Reds	.353
1927	Paul Waner	Pittsburgh Pirates	.380
1928	Rogers Hornsby	Boston Braves	.387
1929	Lefty O'Doul	Philadelphia Phillies	.398
1930	Bill Terry	N.Y. Giants	.401
1931	Chick Hafey	St. Louis Cardinals	.349
1932	Lefty O'Doul	Brooklyn Dodgers	.368
1933	Chuck Klein	Philadelphia Phillies	.368
1934	Paul Waner	Pittsburgh Pirates	.362
1935	Arky Vaughan	Pittsburgh Pirates	.385
1936	Paul Waner	Pittsburgh Pirates	.373
1937	Joe Medwick	St. Louis Cardinals	.374
1938	Ernie Lombardi	Cincinnati Reds	.342
1939	Johnny Mize	St. Louis Cardinals	.349
1940	Debs Garms	Pittsburgh Pirates	.355
1941	Pete Reiser	Brooklyn Dodgers	.343
1942	Ernie Lombardi	Boston Braves	.330

1943	Stan Musial	St. Louis Cardinals	.357
1944	Dixie Walker	Brooklyn Dodgers	.357
1945	Phil Cavarretta	Chicago Cubs	.355
1946	Stan Musial	St. Louis Cardinals	.365
1947	Harry Walker	St. Louis-Philadelphia	.363
1948	Stan Musial	St. Louis Cardinals	.376
1949	Jackie Robinson	Brooklyn Dodgers	.342
1950	Stan Musial	St. Louis Cardinals	.346
1951	Stan Musial	St. Louis Cardinals	.355
1952	Stan Musial	St. Louis Cardinals	.336
1953	Carl Furillo	Brooklyn Dodgers	.344
1954	Willie Mays	N.Y. Giants	.345
1955	Richie Ashburn	Philadelphia Phillies	.338
1956	Hank Aaron	Milwaukee Braves	.328
1957	Stan Musial	St. Louis Cardinals	.351
1958	Richie Ashburn	Philadelphia Phillies	.350
1959	Hank Aaron	Milwaukee Braves	.355
1960	Dick Groat	Pittsburgh Pirates	.325
1961	Roberto Clemente	Pittsburgh Pirates	.351
1962	Tommy Davis	L.A. Dodgers	.346
1963	Tommy Davis	L.A. Dodgers	.326
1964	Roberto Clemente	Pittsburgh Pirates	.339
1965	Roberto Clemente	Pittsburgh Pirates	.329
1966	Matty Alou	Pittsburgh Pirates	.342
1967	Roberto Clemente	Pittsburgh Pirates	.357
1968	Pete Rose	Cincinnati Reds	.335
1969	Pete Rose	Cincinnati Reds	.348
1970	Rico Carty	Atlanta Braves	.366
1971	Joe Torre	St. Louis Cardinals	.363
1972	Billy Williams	Chicago Cubs	.333
1973	Pete Rose	Cincinnati Reds	.338
1974	Ralph Garr	Atlanta Braves	.353
1975	Bill Madlock	Chicago Cubs	.354
1976	Bill Madlock	Chicago Cubs	.339
1977	Dave Parker	Pittsburgh Pirates	.338
1978	Dave Parker	Pittsburgh Pirates	.334

1979	Keith Hernandez	St. Louis Cardinals	.344
1980	Bill Buckner	Chicago Cubs	.324
1981	Bill Madlock	Pittsburgh Pirates	.341
1982	Al Oliver	Montreal Expos	.331
1983	Bill Madlock	Pittsburgh Pirates	.323
1984	Tony Gwynn	San Diego Padres	.351
1985	Willie McGee	St. Louis Cardinals	.353
1986	Tim Raines	Montreal Expos	.334
1987	Tony Gwynn	San Diego Padres	.370
1988	Tony Gwynn	San Diego Padres	.313
1989	Tony Gwynn	San Diego Padres	.336
1990	Willie McGee	St. Louis Cardinals	.335
1991	Terry Pendleton	Atlanta Braves	.319
1992	Gary Sheffield	San Diego Padres	.330
1993	Andres Galarraga	Colorado Rockies	.370
1994	Tony Gwynn	San Diego Padres	.394

WINNERS OF THE ANNUAL ALL-STAR GAME

Year	Winner	Score
1933	American	4–2
1934	American	9–7
1935	American	4–1
1936	National	4–3
1937	American	8–3
1938	National	4–1
1939	American	3–1
1940	National	4–0
1941	American	7–5
1942	American	3–1
1943	American	5–3
1944	National	7–1
1945	No game due to wartime	
1946	American	12–0
1947	American	2–1
1948	American	5–2
1949	American	11–7
1950	National	4–3
1951	National	8–3

WINNERS OF THE ANNUAL ALL-STAR GAME
(continued)

Year	Winner	Score
1952	National	3–2
1953	National	5–1
1954	American	11–9
1955	National	6–5
1956	National	7–3
1957	American	6–5
1958	American	4–3
1959(1)[1]	National	5–4
1959(2)	American	5–3
1960(1)	National	5–3
1960(2)	National	6–0
1961(1)	National	5–4
1961(2)	Tie[2]	1–1
1962(1)	National	3–1
1962(2)	American	9–4
1963	National	5–3
1964	National	7–4
1965	National	6–5
1966	National	2–1
1967	National	2–1
1968	National	1–0
1969	National	9–3
1970	National	5–4
1971	American	6–4
1972	National	4–3
1973	National	7–1
1974	National	7–2
1975	National	6–3
1976	National	7–1
1977	National	7–5
1978	National	7–3

[1]Two All Star games were played 1959–62.
[2]Game was called after nine innings because of rain.

1979	National	7–6
1980	National	4–2
1981	National	5–4
1982	National	4–1
1983	American	13–3
1984	National	3–1
1985	National	6–1
1986	American	3–2
1987	National	2–0
1988	American	2–1
1989	American	5–3
1990	American	2–0
1991	American	4–2
1992	American	13–6
1993	American	9–3
1994	National	9–7

PLAYERS ELECTED TO BASEBALL'S
HALL OF FAME
(Cooperstown, N.Y.)

Aaron, Hank
Alexander, Grover Cleveland
Alston, Walt
Anson, Cap
Aparicio, Luis
Appling, Luke
Averill, Earl
Baker, Home Run
Bancroft, Dave
Banks, Ernie
Barlick, Al
Barrow, Edward G.
Beckley, Jake
Bell, Cool Papa
Bench, Johnny
Bender, Chief
Berra, Yogi
Bottomley, Jim

Boudreau, Lou
Bresnahan, Roger
Brock, Lou
Brouthers, Dan
Brown, Mordecai
  (Three Finger)
Bulkeley, Morgan C.
Burkett, Jesse C.
Campanella, Roy
Carew, Rod
Carey, Max
Carlton, Steve
Cartwright, Alexander
Chadwick, Henry
Chance, Frank
Chandler, Happy
Charleston, Oscar
Chesbro, John

Clarke, Fred

Clarkson, John

Clemente, Roberto

Cobb, Ty

Cochrane, Mickey

Collins, Eddie

Collins, James

Combs, Earle

Comiskey, Charles A.

Conlan, Jocko

Connolly, Thomas H.

Connor, Roger

Coveleski, Stan

Crawford, Sam

Cronin, Joe

Cummings, Candy

Cuyler, Kiki

Dandridge, Ray

Dean, Dizzy

Delahanty, Ed

Dickey, Bill

DiHigo, Martin

DiMaggio, Joe

Doerr, Bobby

Drysdale, Don

Duffy, Hugh

Durocher, Leo

Evans, Billy

Evers, John

Ewing, Buck

Faber, Urban

Feller, Bob

Ferrell, Rick

Fingers, Rollie

Flick, Elmer H.

Ford, Whitey

Foster, Andrew

Foxx, Jimmie

Frick, Ford

Frisch, Frank

Galvin, Pud

Gehrig, Lou

Gehringer, Charles

Gibson, Bob

Gibson, Josh

Giles, Warren

Gomez, Lefty

Goslin, Goose

Greenberg, Hank

Griffith, Clark

Grimes, Burleigh

Grove, Lefty

Hafey, Chick

Haines, Jesee

Hamilton, Bill

Harridge, Will

Harris, Bucky

Hartnett, Gabby

Heilmann, Harry

Herman, Billy

Hooper, Harry

Hornsby, Rogers

Hoyt, Waite

Hubbard, Cal

Hubbell, Carl

Huggins, Miller

Hunter, Catfish

Irvin, Monte

Jackson, Reggie

Jackson, Travis

Jenkins, Ferguson

Jennings, Hugh

Johnson, Byron
Johnson, William (Judy)
Johnson, Walter
Joss, Addie
Kaline, Al
Keefe, Timothy
Keeler, William
Kell, George
Kelley, Joe
Kelly, George
Kelly, King
Killebrew, Harmon
Kiner, Ralph
Klein, Chuck
Klem, Bill
Koufax, Sandy
Lajoie, Napoleon
Landis, Kenesaw M.
Lazzeri, Tony
Lemon, Bob
Leonard, Buck
Lindstrom, Fred
Lloyd, Pop
Lombardi, Ernie
Lopez, Al
Lyons, Ted
Mack, Connie
MacPhail, Larry
Mantle, Mickey
Manush, Henry
Maranville, Rabbit
Marichal, Juan
Marquard, Rube
Mathews, Eddie
Mathewson, Christy
Mays, Willie
McCarthy, Joe
McCarthy, Thomas

McCovey, Willie
McGinnity, Joe
McGowan, Bill
McGraw, John
McKechnie, Bill
Medwick, Joe
Mize, Johnny
Morgan, Joe
Musial, Stan
Newhouser, Hal
Nichols, Kid
O'Rourke, James
Ott, Mel
Paige, Satchel
Palmer, Jim
Pennock, Herb
Perry, Gaylord
Plank, Ed
Radbourn, Charlie
Reese, Pee Wee
Rice, Sam
Rickey, Branch
Rixey, Eppa
Rizzuto, Phil
Roberts, Robin
Robinson, Brooks
Robinson, Frank
Robinson, Jackie
Robinson, Wilbert
Roush, Edd
Ruffing, Red
Rusie, Amos
Ruth, Babe
Schalk, Ray
Schoendienst, Red
Seaver, Tom
Sewell, Joe
Simmons, Al

PLAYERS ELECTED TO BASEBALL'S
HALL OF FAME (continued)

Sisler, George	Walsh, Ed
Slaughter, Enos	Waner, Lloyd
Snider, Duke	Waner, Paul
Spahn, Warren	Ward, John
Spalding, Albert	Weiss, George
Speaker, Tris	Welch, Mickey
Stargell, Willie	Wheat, Zach
Stengel, Casey	Wilhelm, Hoyt
Terry, Bill	Williams, Billy
Thompson, Sam	Williams, Ted
Tinker, Joe	Wilson, Hack
Traynor, Pie	Wright, George
Vance, Dazzy	Wright, Harry
Vaughan, Arky	Wynn, Early
Veeck, Bill	Yastrzemski, Carl
Waddell, Rube	Yawkey, Tom
Wagner, Honus	Young, Cy
Wallace, Roderick	Youngs, Ross

CY YOUNG AWARD WINNERS

1956	Don Newcombe	Brooklyn	NL
1957	Warren Spahn	Milwaukee	NL
1958	Bob Turley	New York	AL
1959	Early Wynn	Chicago	AL
1960	Vernon Law	Pittsburgh	NL
1961	Whitey Ford	New York	AL
1962	Don Drysdale	Los Angeles	NL
1963	Sandy Koufax	Los Angeles	NL
1964	Dean Chance	Los Angeles	AL
1965	Sandy Koufax	Los Angeles	NL
1966	Sandy Koufax	Los Angeles	NL
1967	Jim Lonborg	Boston	AL
	Mike McCormick	San Francisco	NL
1968	Dennis McLain	Detroit	AL
	Bob Gibson	St. Louis	NL

1969	Mike Cuellar	Baltimore	
	Dennis McLain	Detroit	tied in AL
	Tom Seaver	New York	NL
1970	Jim Perry	Minnesota	AL
	Bob Gibson	St. Louis	NL
1971	Vida Blue	Oakland	AL
	Ferguson Jenkins	Chicago	NL
1972	Gaylord Perry	Cleveland	AL
	Steve Carlton	Philadelphia	NL
1973	Jim Palmer	Baltimore	AL
	Tom Seaver	New York	NL
1974	Catfish Hunter	Oakland	AL
	Mike Marshall	Los Angeles	NL
1975	Jim Palmer	Baltimore	AL
	Tom Seaver	New York	NL
1976	Jim Palmer	Baltimore	AL
	Randy Jones	San Diego	NL
1977	Sparky Lyle	New York	AL
	Steve Carlton	Philadelphia	NL
1978	Ron Guidry	New York	AL
	Gaylord Perry	San Diego	NL
1979	Mike Flanagan	Baltimore	AL
	Bruce Sutter	Chicago	NL
1980	Steve Stone	Baltimore	AL
	Steve Carlton	Philadelphia	NL
1981	Rollie Fingers	Milwaukee	AL
	Fernando Valenzuela	Los Angeles	NL
1982	Pete Vuckovich	Milwaukee	AL
	Steve Carlton	Philadelphia	NL
1983	LaMarr Hoyt	Chicago	AL
	John Denny	Philadelphia	NL
1984	Willie Hernandez	Detroit	AL
	Rick Sutcliffe	Chicago	NL
1985	Bret Saberhagen	Kansas City	AL
	Dwight Gooden	New York	NL
1986	Roger Clemens	Boston	AL
	Mike Scott	Houston	NL

CY YOUNG AWARD WINNERS (continued)

Year	Player	Team	League
1987	Roger Clemens	Boston	AL
	Steve Bedrosian	Philadelphia	NL
1988	Frank Viola	Minnesota	AL
	Orel Hershiser	Los Angeles	NL
1989	Bret Saberhagen	Kansas City	AL
	Mark Davis	San Diego	NL
1990	Bob Welch	Oakland	AL
	Doug Drabek	Pittsburgh	NL
1991	Roger Clemens	Boston	AL
	Tom Glavine	Atlanta	NL
1992	Dennis Eckersley	Oakland	AL
	Greg Maddux	Atlanta	NL
1993	Jack McDowell	Chicago	AL
	Greg Maddux	Atlanta	NL
1994	David Cone	Kansas City	AL
	Greg Maddux	Atlanta	NL

TREASURE TROVES OF FACT-FILLED FUN FROM AVON CAMELOT

HOW TO TRAVEL THROUGH TIME
by James M. Deem   76681-7/ $3.50 US/ $4.50 CAN

HOW TO CATCH A FLYING SAUCER
by James M. Deem   71898-7/ $3.50 US/ $4.50 CAN

HOW TO HUNT BURIED TREASURE
by James M. Deem   72176-7/ $3.99 US/ $4.99 CAN

ASK ME ANYTHING ABOUT THE PRESIDENTS
by Louis Phillips   76426-1/ $3.99 US/ $4.99 CAN

ASK ME ANYTHING ABOUT BASEBALL
by Louis Phillips   78029-1/ $3.99 US/ $4.99 CAN

EXPLORING AUTUMN
by Sandra Markle   71910-X/ $3.50 US/ $4.50 CAN

GOBBLE! THE COMPLETE BOOK OF THANKSGIVING WORDS
by Lynda Graham-Barber   71963-0/ $3.99 US/ $4.99 CAN